THE BARCLAYS GUIDE TO

International Trade

for the Small Business

Barclays Small Business Series

Series Editors: Colin Gray and John Stanworth

This new series of highly practical books aimed at new and established small businesses has been written by carefully selected authors in conjunction with the Small Business Unit of Barclays Bank. All the authors have a wide experience of the theory and, more important, the *practice* of small business, and they address the problems that are likely to be encountered by new businesses in a clear and accessible way, including examples and case studies drawn from real business situations.

These comprehensive but compact guides will help owners and managers of small businesses to acquire the skills that are essential if they are to operate successfully in times of rapid change in the business environment.

THE BARCLAYS GUIDE TO

International Trade

Trade

for the Small Business

JOHN WILSON

BARCLAYS
Published by
BLACKWELL

Copyright © John Wilson 1990

First published 1990

Basil Blackwell Ltd
108 Cowley Road, Oxford, OX4 1JF, UK

Basil Blackwell, Inc.
3 Cambridge Center
Cambridge, Massachusetts 02142, USA

British Library Cataloguing in Publication Data
A CIP catalogue record for this book is available from the British Library.

Library of Congress Cataloging in Publication Data
Wilson, John.
The Barclays guide to international trade for the small business /
John Wilson.
p. cm.—(Barclays small business series)
ISBN 0–631–17252–1 (pbk.):
1. International trade—Handbooks, manuals, etc.
2. Small business—Management—Handbooks, manuals, etc.
3. Foreign trade promotion—Handbooks, manuals, etc.
I. Title.   II. Series.
HF1379.W54   1990
658.8'48–dc20   89–18608

Typeset in 10½ on 12½pt Plantin
by Hope Services (Abingdon) Ltd
Printed in Great Britain by
T. J. Press Ltd, Padstow, Cornwall

Contents

Contents

Contents

Foreword

The last five years have seen a significant growth in the number of small businesses in all sectors of industry in the UK. Unfortunately they have also seen an increase in the number of problems encountered by those businesses. Often the problems could have been avoided with the right help and advice.

Barclays, in association with Basil Blackwell, is producing this series of guides to give that help and advice. They are comprehensive and written in a straightforward way. Each one has been written by a specialist in the field, in conjunction with Barclays Bank, and drawing on our joint expertise to ensure that the advice given is appropriate.

With the aid of these guides the businessman or woman will be better prepared to face the many challenges ahead, and, hopefully, will be better rewarded for their efforts.

George Cracknell
Director UK Business
Sector Services
Barclays Bank plc

Acknowledgements

Information and advice was provided by friends, colleagues and the following organizations:

Association of British Chambers of Commerce

Barclays Bank Plc

Chemical Industries Associates

Department of Trade and Industry

Export Network Ltd

Export Opportunities Ltd

Institute of Freight Forwarders

Oldfire Ltd T/A J C Enterprises

London Chamber of Commerce

London Enterprise Agency

MIM Consultants Ltd

Small Business Research Trust

Simpler Trade Procedures Board

Centrepoint Business Services (and Mrs Jill Coogan who not only typed the manuscript but was also most helpful)

Abbreviations

BCC	Business Cooperation Centre
BC-Net	Business Cooperation Network
BHEC	British Health Education Council
BIBA	British Insurance Brokers Association
BOTB	British Overseas Trade Board
BOTIS	British Overseas Trade Information System
BSI	British Standards Institution
BTA	British Tourist Authority
CAD	Cash against documents
CAG	Cash against goods
CCT	Common Customs Tariff
CDA	Cooperative Development Agency
CEDEFOP	European Centre for the Development of Vocational Training
CFR	Cost and freight
CIF	Cost, insurance and freight
CIM	Convention international concernant le transport des merchandises par chemin de fer
CIP	Freight carriage and insurance paid
CMR	Convention relative au contrat de transport international des merchandises par route
COD	Cash on delivery
CPC	Customs Procedure Code
CPT	Freight carriage paid
CRN	Customs Registered Number
DACON	World Bank Data on Consultants
DAF	Delivered at frontier
DDP	Delivered duty paid
DDU	Delivered duty unpaid
DTI	Department of Trade and Industry
EAGGF	European Agricultural Guidance and Guarantee Fund
EC	European Community
ECGD	Export Credits Guarantee Department

ECSC	European Coal and Steel Community
EDI	Electronic data interchange
EDIFACT	Electronic data interchange for Administration, Commerce and Transport
EEC	European Economic Community
EFTA	European Free Trade Association
EIB	European Investment Bank
EIC	European information centre
EIS	Export Intelligence Service
EOL	Export Opportunities Ltd
EPU	Entry processing unit
ERDF	European Regional Development Fund
Euratom	European Atomic Energy Community
EVCA	European Venture Capital Association
EXQ	Ex quay
EXS	Ex ship
EXW	Ex works
FAS	Free alongside ship
FCA	Free carrier
FCL	Full container load
FIATA	International Federation of Forwarding Agents
FLIC	Foreign language courses for industry and commerce
FOB	Free on board
GATT	General Agreement on Tariffs and Trade
GNS	Group of Negotiations on Services
GSP	Generalized System of Preferences
HS	Harmonized Commodity Description and Coding System
IBRD	International Bank for Reconstruction and Development
ICA	International commodity agreements
ICC	International Chamber of Commerce
IDA	International Development Association
IFC	International Finance Corporation
ILB	Industrial lead body
IMP	Integrated Mediterranean Programmes
ITC	International Trade Centre
JETRO	Japan External Trade Organization
LC	Letter of credit

LCL	Less than full container load
LENTA	London Enterprise Agency
LX	Language export
MAR	Marine all risks
NCVQ	National Council for Vocational Qualifications
NVQ	National Vocational Qualification
OECD	Organization for Economic Cooperation and Development
PDS	Product Data Store
PICKUP	Professional, Industrial and Commercial Updating Programme
RO/RO	Roll on and roll off
SAD	Single Administrative Document
SEA	Single European Act
SITPRO	Simpler Trade Procedures Board
SME	Small and medium-sized enterprises
SSN	Standard shipping note
TEEM	TransEurope Express Merchandise
THE	Technical Help for Exporters
TVA	Taxe sur la valeur ajoutée
UN/TDI	United Nations Guidelines for Trade Data Interchange
UNCTAD	United Nations Conference on Trade and Development
VAT	Value-added tax

Introduction

International trade is essential for the maintenance and growth of prosperity in all countries. It is particularly important for the UK which needs to import many of its raw materials which in turn can only be paid for by exports. Much government effort is spent on encouraging companies to engage in exporting or to increase exports. However, still far too few business and management training courses include the managing of an international business as an essential part of the course. Those engaged in the direction and management of small and medium-sized enterprises (SMEs) are least likely to have had any formal training to do with the management of exporting and importing.

This book sets out to assist those thinking of starting or already engaged in running a small business. It will help them to assess the opportunities in international trade and how they might profitably exploit these opportunities. It will also be of use to those in larger companies who wish to know more about the management and administration of exporting and importing.

The development of the single market creates a need for all directors and managers to know how to do business with companies in Europe and how to compete with other organizations in and from Europe as well as with their traditional UK rivals. Marketing and sales staff must become equipped to operate in the new market environment. Hopefully the bureaucratic obstacles to trade within the European Community will disappear and it will only be necessary to overcome the language and cultural barriers.

The communications revolution over the last 50 years means that time and distance barriers to trade hardly exist in most situations. The telephone, fax and telex, with satellite cable and radio links, have made it possible for business people in all the great cities of the world to speak or to send documents to one another directly with minimum delays. The growth of air freight and containerization has facilitated the movement of goods so that within Western Europe the less bulky and lighter goods can be delivered within 48 hours of despatch. Add to this the speed with which the air freight industry

1

can move goods between continents and it is apparent that in theory business can be done with customers and suppliers overseas almost as easily as if they were within the UK.

The great advance in the efficiency of communications and the development of information databases has made it far simpler for exporters to obtain information on potential markets. Similarly importers can readily obtain knowledge of foreign suppliers and of their goods and services. It is also much easier to obtain details of new inventions, new products and improved merchandise available in the developed countries in Western Europe, North America and the Far East. Access to global information is becoming more and more essential if companies are to grow and succeed in today's environment.

This book deals with both exporting and importing. To be good at one it is necessary to know about the other. The seller should know about the problems of the buyer and the buyer about those of the seller. Any company that has a product or service to sell which is of possible interest to overseas customers ought to investigate the possibility of export sales. Similarly if it knows of a new product or service in its field available in an overseas market which could be marketed in the UK it should investigate the possibility of selling here and then perhaps in other overseas markets. However, unless the company already has a good understanding of international trade it would be most unwise to start up or extend its business simply on the basis of some market research. Selling and buying where you are domiciled is much easier than selling or buying abroad. This will change as the single market becomes more and more a reality and obstacles to trading within the EC disappear. Companies will have to forget the strip of water that separates us from the continent and recognize that, for trading, such places as Paris are much nearer to them than many towns in the UK. Competition within the UK from small firms on the continent will also increase as buyers here see the opportunities to purchase supplies from Community countries. Similarly opportunities for British firms to sell in Western Europe will increase.

Many people and organizations delight in explaining how difficult and complex it is to export. This is undoubtedly true if you are trying to sell in a developing country which is short of sterling or other hard currencies (i.e. currencies which are freely exchangeable).

If they also lack a good infrastructure in such areas as transport and banking facilities and erect obstacles to overseas trading then even more difficulties arise and considerable knowledge, skill and ingenuity is required to overcome them.

Exporting, and indeed importing, is not difficult if you are intending to sell or buy in a developed country with a freely exchangeable and stable currency, well-structured financial, industrial and retail sectors, good transport facilities and few obstacles to overseas trade. If you choose wisely where and how to start trading it will be a lot less difficult than you might imagine.

To run any successful business it is necessary to develop the right knowledge, skills and expertise not only to manage certain aspects of it oneself but also to be able to employ or make use of outside experts when necessary. Sales and marketing skills are essential in any small business. It is not sufficient to have a background of knowledge and experience only of the home market if you wish to engage in international trade. Gaining knowledge and skills for overseas trading by experience can be very expensive as a number of small firms have found to their cost.

A number of entrepreneurs have built up their basic knowledge of overseas trade by reading appropriate books and magazines and by attending a number of short courses run by such organizations as the Chambers of Commerce. Even if you intend to employ an experienced export sales manager it is still essential to have an overall understanding of the methods and mechanisms of inter-national trading. Too many small and medium-sized enterprises (SMEs) enter into overseas trading because an overseas buyer approaches them with an order or a salesman from an overseas supplier makes an interesting offer. If you engage in an overseas trade transaction without prior knowledge of the possible pitfalls you may be lucky and successful. Too often small firms are not successful, having failed to realize that overseas business needs to be dealt with in a systematic manner covering all aspects of quality, payment, insurance, packaging, transport and delivery, and the relevant documentation. It is even more important to remember that in overseas trading you have not made a sale until you have been paid nor have you completed your purchase until you have taken the title and physical possession of the goods to your satisfaction.

The development of the single market has important implications for your company if you expect to do business as a buyer and/or seller beyond your local community. UK companies of all sizes will be quick to seize any advantage from buying from companies outside the UK, especially if the supplier is located in mainland Europe. Unfortunately many are unlikely to be as quick to seize the advantages of selling their products throughout the single market. If your company is buying and/or selling nationally then in order to survive in the 1990s you should gradually extend your coverage to all the countries in the EC. In learning to trade now with companies in mainland Europe you will acquire knowledge and experience which will also enable you to develop business with other parts of the world such as the USA.

The first step in exporting is to identify the customers and markets that could be interested in your product. You must then find out with which of these you can hope to do business at a profit. There is no point in spending time, money and effort in trying to sell in a particular market or to a customer unless there is every likelihood that you will make a satisfactory profit. There are a variety of ways in which you can carry out some quick market research to obtain information which will enable you to decide where and how to concentrate your initial efforts. These will be described later in this book. Unfortunately many firms drift into exporting or importing because they make contact with a buyer or seller at an exhibition or through receiving enquiries or offers. This is not the best way to enter into international trade. It is far better to approach it in a systematic manner having thought out your strategy and developed plans to acquire the knowledge, skills, contacts and help that will enable you to be successful.

There are many organizations in the UK who will assist you to trade internationally; many, such as government departments, the major banks and central public libraries, provide free information and some free services. There is an increasing amount of education and training available, some at low cost, from the educational sector as well as from bodies such as the Chambers of Commerce, professional institutes and commercial organizations. Many are endeavouring to promote their seminars, in order to earn some revenue for their organizations as well as to provide a service to their members, subscribers and, usually at a higher price, non-members.

The successful international trader is also fully aware of the need to understand the language and cultural differences that exist not only between countries but also between different parts of the same country. Although English is generally the language of international trade it is of definite advantage to a seller to be able to communicate with a buyer in the buyer's own native language. This is very apparent in the EC where, for example, French buyers will generally expect you to be able to speak some French. Cultural differences must also be understood because sales can be lost and have been lost by making cultural errors and offending the potential customer. The old adage about the need to know your buyer has a much wider meaning when you engage in international trade.

The language and cultural barriers are a reason why some SMEs prefer indirect exporting to direct exporting. Indirect exporting involves using export marketing agents or export trading houses in the UK who will develop your exports for you. In some industries, small companies obtain indirect exports by supplying equipment to main contractors and major manufacturers for their overseas as well as their UK business. Similarly, importers often buy products made overseas from UK wholesalers and stockists rather than buying them directly from manufacturers abroad.

It does not matter whether you are a potential exporter or importer: if you intend to engage to any significant extent in international trade, you should evaluate the existing resources within your business before you make the commitment. This is the subject of the next chapter. Subsequent chapters explain the different key aspects of international trade. The appendices provide a comprehensive list of information sources with addresses and telephone, telex and fax numbers.

I

Evaluating your business for international trade

Outline

To begin in international trade you will need to know the capabilities of your business very well. This chapter will help you to evaluate:

- the information flow in the business
- your production capacity
- your sales and marketing resources
- the suitability of your packaging and labelling
- your financial capacity
- the plans you will need to draw up
- the market research you will need to do

No matter how small or large your business, it is essential to evaluate the resources you have available to support your entry into international trade. You need to determine your company's strengths and weaknesses and decide where you will need to use outside help. It is also necessary to think ahead and have not only budgets and forecasts but also a business plan which incorporates all aspects of your business and the way you expect it to develop. Make sure your plans include not only specific figures, e.g. sales targets, but also less tangible judgements about for example the level of skills required. For a small firm it is not necessary to have sophisticated and complex plans. It is important to have plans that you understand and can pursue and modify when necessary in response to your progress and actual experience.

It is best to review your resources under various headings although more than one aspect of your business is likely to be looked after by one person. Choose headings as you wish, but you will probably find that most of the following will be helpful to you.

Information

It is recognized that one of the ways to success in any business is to have an adequate flow of information about how it is progressing. You need to have continuously not only your own internal management control information but also external information about your markets, your customers, your suppliers and much else to enable your company to perform efficiently. In international trade you are operating in continuously changing environments, e.g. with moving exchange rates, and it is important for the relevant people in your organization to keep themselves up to date with what is happening.

Determine first what your staff and you know about international trading. Do your marketing and sales people know where to obtain information about overseas markets? Do they know organizations in the UK from which they can obtain not only information but also help and advice? Has your company the right contacts for banking, insurance, shipping and documentation assistance?

If you know very little about international trade your central library and local booksellers will have suitable books to enable you to learn much about exporting or importing before you become seriously involved. It is hoped that this book will provide you with much of the information you need. You can also increase your knowledge and that of your staff by attending seminars on specific aspects of overseas trade.

Production

At some point in your planning you will be making an estimate of probable sales. Even before you make such an estimate, you should determine how much spare production capacity you have or could create for your export business. There is no point in thinking about exporting unless you have spare capacity or can afford to buy additional capacity. It is not only equipment that you have to consider but also the number of people you will need to make your overseas orders.

Increasingly countries have regulations governing the technical contents or use of a product. Satisfy yourselves that you have sufficient flexibility in your production to be able to produce to different standards and that you have the necessary company skills to make technical changes.

If you are importing, ensure that the product you propose to import meets UK technical requirements and that you have the appropriate warehouse capacity to handle your imports.

Sales and marketing

The small firm that has staff with export sales and marketing skills as well as export office skills is indeed fortunate. It is essential to have someone who can develop an expertise in overseas sales and marketing and who can learn how to motivate and manage agents. This member of staff also needs to be able to deal with all the administrative aspects in conjunction with someone who understands export documentation. In the smallest firms one person will probably have responsibility for all aspects of exporting assisted by a secretary. In larger companies with more overseas business one person needs to be a specialist in sales and marketing and the other in documentation. If necessary much of the documentation can be handled by a freight forwarder or an outside specialist providing a documentary service. Review your existing resources and decide how you wish to develop this key aspect of your export business. Do not forget that you will also require a source of language expertise. Identify any foreign language skills, both written and verbal, possessed by your staff and an outside language service that you can use. As you develop in the Common Market you will need to have a source of language skills in French, German, Spanish and Italian as your minimum requirements for communication and translation.

If you are intending to import, your needs will not be as great as those of an exporter; nevertheless someone needs to develop the appropriate buying and documentation expertise which may perhaps already exist to some extent amongst your staff.

Packaging and labelling

Export packing can be a major problem if you have sensitive or fragile products. See whether you have the necessary knowledge within your organization; if not, find out where you can obtain it. Not only do you have to pack exports suitably but you must also be aware of the labelling requirements. You will need to know the United Nations (UN) agreed formats for labelling – these are available from the Simpler Trade Procedures Board (SITPRO) (see appendix 5). All this will involve additional work so make sure that your employees who do these operations will have time to do them! Specialist export packing companies can be employed or your freight forwarder can advise of the packaging and labelling requirements for each market.

but nevertheless he will need someone to ensure that imported goods arrive correctly addressed and suitably packed.

Finance

The major concern in any small business is to be able to manage its affairs, particularly its finances, efficiently and profitably. Exporting will have a major impact on your business and you need to consider whether you have the financial resources and the financial expertise to cope with the demands of exporting.

An initial investment may be required to develop your export sales. You will also need to estimate the effect of exporting on your cash flow and working capital. Have you sufficient financial resources within the company to support your development plans? Will your existing financial backers give you more support or will you need to find new financial support?

In most small firms the person looking after the accounts is probably also responsible for receiving customer's payments and for paying bills for purchased products and services. If you have someone concerned with the accounts who is already familiar with the international trade payment methods as well as with the different types of documentary bills that arise from exporting, you have a valuable resource. Should you not have this resource you will need to acquire it, either by giving one of your staff some suitable training or by acquiring outside help.

There are various methods of improving your cash flow from exports if you have to grant credit, and you should seek your bank's advice. Methods such as discounting bills, factoring of debts and forfaiting should all be known to a member of your accounts staff. In particular he should know how to check upon the credit worthiness of customers and how to chase and collect bad debts from overseas as well as UK customers.

If you are proposing to import instead of export then you will still need to look at your financial resources, especially if you intend to hold stocks of the imported goods or have to provide credit to your buyers for longer than you are able to obtain it from your supplier. You will also need in-house knowledge about the various methods of payment and insurance.

People and fixed assets

The success of your whole business – not just your exporting – depends vitally on the quality and skills of the people you employ. In evaluating all your resources it is essential to review the knowledge and skills (including language skills) of all your staff. Assess whether or not they are likely to be able to acquire some skills relating to exporting and prepare a training plan. Recruit new staff where necessary or arrange to use outside services, e.g. for documentation.

Have a look at your fixed assets to ensure that you have sufficient space for the expansion of your business. Is your building large enough and have you the space to cope with increased production, more packaging and more documentation? Will you need more machines for production and more equipment for your offices? At what point in the expansion of your business might you need to move to new premises? Material resources are as vital as people resources if your business is to become an effective international trader.

Planning

In any business it is essential to have plans, to monitor your progress against these plans and to adjust them in the light of actual results.

Your overall business development plan will cover the four major areas of your business – finance, production, marketing and people. Developing an international trade dimension to your business will have an impact on all four areas but particularly the marketing area. Your marketing plan needs to focus on several subsidiary areas. See what resources you have available to carry them out and then decide how they will be undertaken. The four subsidiary areas are as follows.

market research: desk and field

selling: management and methods

administration: documentation, systems and controls

product: specifications, packaging, labelling and instructions

We will look at market research in chapter 2, selling in chapters 3 to 5 and administration in chapter 6.

In a small firm it is essential to have clear targets and to be confident about how you intend to try to achieve them. Thinking ahead is all-important; otherwise your responses to customers' requirements, competition and other changes may be too late.

Product plan

It is probable that many small firms can develop and implement most aspects of a product plan from their own resources. Evaluating the production capacity and managing production for export is unlikely to require outside assistance. However, if assistance is required to determine the technical requirements for a particular market this information can be obtained from Technical Help for Exporters (THE), a branch of the British Standards Institution (BSI). Similarly the British Design Council can advise on design requirements in different countries (see appendix 13 for addresses). Also it is important to know whether certain colours are unacceptable as well as differences in size requirements. It may be necessary to have a special product range for export. The product plan should include provision for all instructions for using the product especially any that may be fixed to the product during production to be in appropriate foreign languages.

Having determined what changes will be necessary to meet export requirements, the product cost should be established. It is also important to be aware of the relationship between your costs and volume of production so that you will know when your business will break even.

The following is a summary of some of the points you should consider in preparing your product plan.

product range
production capacity
technical specifications
design and styling
packaging and labelling
usage instructions in foreign languages
product cost
cost and production volume relationship

Should you be planning to be an importer it is still necessary to have a product plan which covers many of the same aspects as an exporter would consider. You will need to discuss many of these points with your overseas supplier, but in addition you will need to consider such matters as suppliers' delivery schedules and your own warehousing, repacking and relabelling facilities.

Key points

- Good accurate information is the key to doing business internationally.
- Make sure you evaluate your resources carefully to ensure that you are able to deal effectively with overseas suppliers and customers.
- When preparing your business plan make sure you consider fully the nature of the product/service; the management, training and outside support you will need; capital expenditure; the markets and how you will reach them; and the financial issues – how much capital you will need, cash flow forecasts and a break-even analysis.
- You need a plan for success.

2

Market research

Outline

Successful international trading depends upon thorough market intelligence. This chapter explains the various types of research you can undertake including:

- desk and field research
- visiting your export markets
- researching for importers

This short chapter should be read in conjunction with appendix 20 which gives details of the relevant sources of information. Recent research shows that, of 12,000 manufacturers with a turnover of £1 million to £10 million only, a quarter were active exporters, another quarter were passive exporters and the remainder did no direct exporting. While it is clearly possible to be a passive exporter, just waiting for overseas buyers to find you and place orders, it is not an efficient way to develop your business. With the advent of the single market, passive exporters are likely to find themselves at a distinct disadvantage to their competitors from Western Europe who are active exporters. Similar considerations apply to importers who are not actively concerned to evaluate products from manufacturers in other Common Market countries.

Market research for exporting

Market research is a systematic way of obtaining information about your existing and potential markets. In order to be a successful exporter it is necessary to carry out market research as a continuous commitment. However, a major market research effort will be required before you enter a new market or introduce new products. There are various market research organizations who will carry out specific research for a fee, but the Department of Trade and Industry (DTI) offers subsidized help. Under the Enterprise Initiative a company can receive part funding of the services of a marketing consultancy for up to 15 days' consultancy which will provide them with a market strategy for their UK and overseas business. The Association of British Chambers of Commerce run the DTI's Export Market Research Scheme which is open to any firm that wishes to research the overseas prospects for its UK manufactured products or its UK-based services. Their Export Market Research advisers offer free professional advice on how to do the research. If you wish to employ professional researchers or use your own in-house experts, financial support is available under the scheme.

Nineteen Chambers of Commerce and the Export Enterprise Centres in Essex and Kent operate the DTI's Active Exporting Scheme (see appendix 7) which helps companies evaluate the export potential for their products. The initial assistance will be either free or at a reduced fee to help formulate an initial plan involving the use of information services. To obtain more information about, and application forms for, any of the above schemes apply to your nearest DTI regional office (see appendix 3).

Desk research

Many small firms will feel that employing a market researcher is too expensive for them and will look for wider help and advice such as is available under the DTI's Enterprise Initiative Marketing Consultancy scheme. However, it is possible to undertake the desk and field research yourself. The experience of doing it is invaluable since it will help you to know how to keep yourself up to date with what is happening in your markets. Clearly the first step to take if you are doing the desk research yourself is to find out who are the information providers and to formulate the questions to ask to get at the information you are seeking. Broadly you will need information on markets, competitors, competitive products and potential agents, distributors and customers. There are a number of very important sources of information which you will need to contact and details of some of these are given in appendix 20.

Field research

Once you have completed your desk research and decided which markets you wish to tackle first, you will probably need to visit your chosen markets in order to obtain more information and to meet potential agents, distribution stockists and customers. In general it is best to pick a few markets for your initial efforts. For example you might start with France, Germany, Holland and Belgium and then extend to Spain, Portugal and Italy before tackling the Scandinavian countries or those such as Greece, Austria and Switzerland. Some writers will recommend that you should only choose one country for your initial efforts but the disadvantage of this approach is that it may prove a much more difficult country in which to find an agent or to sell your product than you expect. If you endeavour to build up your business in a few countries simultaneously it is likely that you will succeed quickly in one of the countries. Naturally there is no reason for beginning your exporting in Europe if your market research shows that the USA, Japan, Commonwealth countries or any other parts of the world appear to offer you the greatest potential for profitable business and you can see clearly how you might develop it.

Visit plan

Every time you visit your markets it is essential to work to a pre-arranged plan. Make appointments particularly with your potential agents and customers before you go, so that your time will be used most effectively. Arrange to see the commercial section of the British diplomatic post, in order to check out some of the information you have already obtained and perhaps get some more. Contact the British Chamber of Commerce in the market (see appendix 9) as in some countries such as the Netherlands, Germany and France they are particularly helpful. A visit to the foreign branch or the correspondent bank branch of your UK bank will often provide you with up-to-date information on any likely payment delays or other problems. If you can also arrange to meet some representatives of other UK companies in the markets this could be especially valuable. Should you be selling retail products then do visit shops and stores to find out what competitive products are being sold and how they are priced. Do this before you visit any potential agents or customers. If you are visiting a non-English-speaking market, make sure you have a translator available to assist you in the market. The DTI or the Chamber of Commerce will assist you to find one.

Trade missions

One of the best ways to visit markets outside the single market is to join a trade mission. This reduces the cost of the visit as they are normally subsidized. You will also be travelling with experienced exporters who will usually be delighted to give you some help and advice. Discuss with your Chamber of Commerce what you want to achieve with your visit, i.e. your target and how you think you should set about it. The mission leader should be able to guide you and help you arrange meetings in advance. If you are visiting a non-English-speaking country, make sure there will be a translator available to assist you. Remember that on your first visit you are going out to check information, make some successful business contacts and possibly do some business.

Travel plan

The experienced traveller is someone who knows most of the pitfalls of overseas travel. Flight delays are something with which everyone is now familiar but in some developing countries they can be much worse than they are in the UK. Make sure you have a reliable travel agent with representatives in the countries you propose to visit. Your travel agent should advise you about the documents you require, e.g. visas and carnets if you are taking in samples. He should also warn you of the health risks and the vaccinations which are compulsory and those which are desirable. Check with the British Airways Travel Clinics or a Yellow Fever Vaccination Centre in your area (see appendix 15) or with your local doctor as they will have leaflets explaining what is required for each country and will arrange for you to be immunized.

A good travel agent should also be able to advise you about clothing requirements and travel from the airport to your hotel. In some countries, unless your travel agent has a representative in the market you may be shocked to discover that you have no hotel booking when you get to the reception desk. Sadly hotels do overbook and in addition there may be some local customs that your travel agent's representative has to satisfy before your reservation is firmly held for you. If the travel agent's representative meets you at the airport and accompanies you to your hotel you are reasonably certain that you will have a hotel room. In some countries this is essential.

Unfortunately you can also have difficulties in getting through airport formalities and in changing your traveller's cheques to the local currency, e.g. if you can only exchange money at certain hours. In the case of Western European countries, North America, Japan and other hard currency countries, there should be no problems and in any case you can always buy some local currency in the UK before your departure. It is in developing countries with exchange controls that you need to know about the problems in advance of your visit.

Your desk research should have enabled you to decide which markets offer the best potential for the least difficulty. It should also have enabled you to determine how your competitors or those selling products complementary to yours actually do sell their products in each market and the prices at which they are sold. Hopefully you will also have identified some agents, distributors, stockists and buyers. There is much other useful information which you should have gathered during the course of the research. In addition you should have established some useful personal contacts who will give you help and advice when you require further information or have some problems to solve. Nevertheless you are unlikely to have obtained all the marketing and sales information you require even if you have also had some professional market research carried out on your chosen markets. At this stage you will also have realized that there is a great deal more to learn about the administration and mechanics of exporting. Sources of information and help for this area of your business activity are dealt with in a later chapter.

Market research for importing

If you are intending to be an importer and wish to look at new markets, possible new products from abroad and new overseas suppliers you will wish to undertake market research to find out your best sources of supply.

The commercial sections of foreign embassies in the UK will provide you with information on their country's exports including lists of products and lists of possible suppliers. Write to these suppliers for the fullest information about their companies, their products, prices, terms and sales, methods of delivery, length of time for delivery and any other information relevant to your business. If necessary ask for samples of their products. Pay particular attention to the specifications you agree with the supplier as without a proper specification you may find yourself receiving some inferior goods.

Foreign trade associations and Chambers of Commerce in London, such as the Portuguese Chamber of Commerce and Industry in the UK, will provide you with much useful information to enable you to find suppliers to meet your needs (see appendix 8). Some of these Chambers of Commerce organize trade missions of buyers to enable them to make contacts with appropriate manufacturers. Also a number of Chambers of Commerce both in the UK and in overseas countries supply lists of manufacturers looking for UK agents and importers.

The Developing Countries Trade Agency helps developing countries promote their international trade through special studies and projects in selected industries. Importers should register their interests in certain products from specified countries with the Trade Agency as it is possible that it can give the importer some useful information.

Statistics and general information on overseas markets can be obtained from many of the same sources as the exporter would use in carrying out his market research.

Key points

- Market research is an essential part of your planning for international trade – make sure that you invest the necessary time and resources.
- Try to visit overseas suppliers if you are importing and travel your markets if you plan to export.
- Make full use of all the available sources of information.
- Don't ignore the results of your market research!

3

Sales planning

Outline

This chapter will help you to set realistic and achievable sales targets. It explains:

- different methods of selling overseas
- supporting and communicating with agents
- sales promotion materials
- how to establish a sales unit
- how to prepare detailed sales plans

Our initial overall sales plan involving every market and individual products should cover a number of aspects such as

methods of selling
promoting sales
maintaining a sales unit
pricing structures
payment terms
delivery systems
sales staff

Payment issues are dealt with in chapter 4, delivery systems in chapter 5 and staff in chapter 6. Here we concentrate on methods of selling and promotion.

Methods of selling

In establishing a sales plan you must decide which methods of selling and sales promotion you intend to use in your chosen markets. This will depend to some extent on the established methods used successfully by others and the cost of different methods. No two markets will be exactly alike, nor will the selling methods necessarily be the same for different industries or retail sectors. The following are the most likely methods of selling:

agents, distributors and stockists
cooperative trading
direct selling to overseas companies
representatives of foreign buyers in the UK
trading houses
fairs and exhibitions

Agents, distributors and stockists

One of the aspects of exporting that causes most problems to exporting companies of all sizes is finding and appointing good agents. Always endeavour to find at least two and preferably three potential agents for the area to be covered. The area can be the whole country, e.g. France, or part of a country, e.g. the East Coast of the USA, or a group of countries, e.g. Belgium and Holland. Be careful to ensure that the proposed agent really can cover the territory you wish to allocate to him. Do not expect him to cover the whole of West Germany if that is not the normal practice of agents in that country. Always visit the potential agents before you decide which one to appoint. Check on their credit worthiness to ensure they are of reasonable financial strength and obtain references, one of which should be from their bank and another from the trade.

Finding agents

Considerable effort may be required to find an agent and more than one method may have to be tried such as

advertising in the national or trade press of the overseas market
writing to agents identified from directories
advertising at exhibitions
making personal contacts at trade fairs and conferences
seeking help from your local bank, the local Chamber of Commerce, the UK Chamber of Commerce overseas, the overseas Chamber of Commerce in the UK or the regional office of the DTI

Always try to meet your potential agents at their offices and ware-houses. See for yourself what facilities they have available and what other products they are stocking if you are appointing them to act as your stockist.

Appointing agents

Small firms are often reluctant to have formal agreements with their agents. Agent, distributor and stockist agreements should define the responsibilities of each party and always include an arbitration clause and a clause stating how the parties to the agreement may terminate the contract. An example of an agreement which can be used as the basis for drawing up agency agreements is given in appendix 2. However, you will need to think out your own clauses for inclusion in the agreement and you should have it checked by a lawyer who is experienced in international trade before submitting it to your agents. This is important because the laws relating to agency agreements vary considerably from country to country. In some you can be legally liable for large compensation payments when you terminate the agreement.

Supporting the agent

When you are appointing your agents, distributors or stockists you should also decide how you intend to support them, to communicate with them and to monitor their activities. Simply appointing an agent does not automatically result in business. In fact you may find with experience you have appointed the wrong agent and then you must terminate the agreement at least cost. However, very few agents will be effective unless you support them actively, are regularly in contact with them, meet them face to face and monitor their performance.

The same comments are relevant if you are an importer because it is to your benefit to get the best out of your suppliers. Whether you are exporting or importing you should agree a forward sales plan with your overseas agent or a purchasing/supply forecast with your overseas supplier.

The sales plan agreed with an overseas agent should not only include target sales figures but how the agent intends to promote your product. He will require information and advertising copy as well as art and design work if he is to translate and produce his promotional material locally. However, it is more than likely that you will have to supply the agent with brochures, leaflets etc. already translated into the local language. You will also need to agree on the number of samples or the amount of demonstration equipment he will require. The latter need not be free if he is able to sell it. If he has sales representatives you may have to agree to provide them with some training so they will be more effective in promoting and answering questions about your product. At all times you should keep your agent informed of delivery periods so that his delivery promises to the customers are realistic. In turn he should send you regular reports about the market, competition and any other matters which will help you. You should send him news-letters, keep him up to date with your sales ideas and provide him with successful sales stories.

If you are an importer your prime concerns will be quality, delivery and price. These should be stated in detail on every order you place with your supplier. If possible give him an estimate of your forward requirements and advise immediately whenever you need to change them. In turn he should give you his actual and estimated delivery schedules so that you will know when to expect material that has been ordered as well as the availability of further supplies.

Communicating

It is important to agree with your overseas sales agents or overseas suppliers which language you will use for communicating. As English is generally recognized as the language of international business it is not unreasonable to expect to be able to use English. However, you should be willing to communicate in their local language especially if your competitors do so. Within the single market countries as in other countries of the world you must be willing to sell and communicate in the language of the buyer. Fortunately most major international buyers are willing to use English so do not be deterred if you do not have a particular language skill within your organiza-tion. You can use translation services in the UK and translators in the market for your visit. However, always determine in advance of any visit or meeting whether English is acceptable to the buyer and if not whether another language such as French or German is acceptable. SMEs in many foreign language markets are unlikely to be able to communicate satisfactorily with you in English. There are language and cultural barriers to be overcome in dealing with all overseas territories but sensible planning will enable you to overcome these barriers.

Make sure you have the means to communicate with your agent, i.e. by telephone, telex, facsimile, post and courier. Do ensure that someone in your organization maintains regular personal contact with him by telephone and by the occasional visit, e.g. once a year. Obviously the more business you do in a market the more support you can give the agent and the more frequently you can visit him. Never go to an overseas market without planning your visit in advance and be clear about what you are trying to achieve. Naturally on each visit you will discuss with your agent his past sales performance, his major existing and potential customers, the general sales strategy, competition and any problems relating to the product, packing, delivery and price. In addition you should discuss the general market conditions and especially the financial situation and how payments in foreign currency and exchange rates might be affected. Finally you will need to agree a forward sales plan. You should expect a commitment from your agent to at least achieve the sales forecast and he will expect a similar commitment from you on supplies and deliveries.

Cooperative trading

Cooperative trading whereby two or more companies work together to market their products in the UK and overseas is a well-established method of trading in the agricultural products industry. The arrangements whereby companies come together to assist each other with their sales and marketing vary considerably but usually they form a joint marketing company or agency. The Cooperative Development Agency (CDA) can advise you if there are any organizations in your product area that you could join in such a venture.

Another form of trading is that developed by some multinationals, notably ICI. The ICI Tradeway system enables companies making products complementary but not competitive to those of ICI to use

ICI trading companies overseas as their agents. The worldwide network operates from London and your initial approach would be to them but once a sales office overseas has agreed to act as your agent you would liaise directly with that office. The local sales offices will

- provide you with detailed information about the market and financing conditions
- quickly learn about your products and assess their opportunities
- have close contact with your potential customers
- know the laws, language, documentation requirements and customs of the country
- monitor progress, identify new openings and offer market advice for your products

It will be necessary to enter into an agency agreement with the local sales office and agree sales commissions. If they are to act as your local stockist it will also be necessary to agree such matters as payment terms, stock levels and replenishment times.

Direct selling

The number of potential customers in a market or group of markets, your expected frequency of sales, the type of product you sell and the size and value of orders should influence your choice of method of selling. If you have only a few large potential customers then it may be possible to sell to them by direct visits from the UK. Alternatively you could appoint an individual who lives in the area to be your salesman or sales representative for an overseas country. The individual would probably expect to be paid a salary or retainer fee, plus a commission and expenses. Valid expense items need to be precisely defined in order to avoid conflicts.

There is an increase in the number of company salesmen travelling from the UK to sell direct to customers on the European mainland and there are individuals acting as commission salesmen in the single market selling for groups of small firms selling complementary products.

Representatives of overseas companies in the UK

A number of overseas companies, especially large retail houses, maintain buying offices in the UK. The DTI regional offices are able to supply a list of these offices which are mainly situated in London. There are also buying agents in London for some large overseas companies and the DTI regional office, your trade association and your local Chamber of Commerce should be able to provide you with some addresses.

It should not be forgotten that multinationals with headquarters in the UK often act as buyers for their overseas subsidiaries and associates. They may also lay down technical specifications for certain products used throughout the group. If your products fall into this category then ensure that they are approved technically by the appropriate department within the group. This situation will apply to some other multinationals with headquarters in other countries such as West Germany, France, Switzerland and the USA. International directories can be consulted to determine the names of multinational companies who are possible buyers of your product.

Trading houses

Using a trading house means exporting by proxy. The advantage of using a trading house is that it takes many of the problems of exporting out of your hands. The disadvantage to the manufacturer is that he may become very dependent on the trading house for his business, he may not get to know the overseas markets and the consumers of his goods and he may not have control over the final price to the customer. However, the value of using a trading house to begin exporting or for exporting to some parts of the world or certain trade and industry sectors should not be underestimated.

There are a number of different types of trading houses. Manufacturer's export agents sell a company's goods in selected markets under their own name or under that of the manufacturer. In effect the export agent acts as the export arm of the manufacturer, saving the manufacturer from a considerable direct investment in people with export skills.

Export merchants who buy on their own account and then sell abroad are acting like any other wholesaler. There are many such companies in every country acting as either export or import merchants and they are very common in the retail goods sector especially in the textile garment field. ICI Chance & Hunt is an outstanding example of an international chemical merchanting and trading house of great help to many manufacturers.

Confirming houses are different from other trading houses in that they have an agency relationship with foreign companies who they represent and who pay them on a commission basis. The confirming house usually buys from the manufacturer on a direct contract of sale and is liable for the payment and acceptance of the goods. Alternatively he may place an order on behalf of the overseas customer but be responsible for the price, and payment if the buyer defaults.

The British Exporters Association publishes a directory of its members and markets and services offered, including products handled by its members (see appendix 18).

Exhibitions, fairs and conferences

Small firms should always consider participating in the major international exhibitions, trade fairs and conferences in their industrial or product area. At the right exhibition it is possible to make contacts with a large number of potential customers and to find some potential overseas agents. It is essential to attend only the exhibitions and trade fairs where you will obtain a good return. Exhibition organizers will impress you with their sales promotion material but find out from your customers, other manufacturers in your industry and your trade association which are likely to be the most important international exhibitions for you. Attending the exhibition will also help you to know more about your competitors.

The major international exhibitions and trade fairs are both in the UK and overseas. Some overseas trade fairs will be important for your agent. You should discuss with him his possible participation and give him the necessary support; providing it will assist him to promote your product in his market.

The DTI Fairs and Promotions Branch as well as your trade association should be able to give you details of forthcoming exhibitions and trade fairs in your field. There are also directories published listing the forthcoming major fairs and exhibitions. In addition Export Network Ltd have information about them in their on-line database.

Seminars and conferences especially if they are spread over two or three days also provide opportunities for making sales contacts and sometimes sales. If you are in a technical industry they can be important platforms for promoting the technical quality of your product. One small firm making dental materials has been highly successful in developing their export business simply by attending international conferences for dentists.

Promoting sales

Once you have decided on your methods of selling it is also necessary to decide on your sales promotion materials. If you are selling to a non-English-speaking country then all your material will have to be translated into the local language and checked, preferably by your agent. Translation, especially of brand names and descriptions, can result in words which are not acceptable locally; similarly, certain colours may give the wrong impression, as can some logos and designs. If you wish to find translators ask your local Chamber of Commerce or LX centre; if they cannot find an appropriate person the Institute of Linguists or the Institute of Translators and Interpreting should be able to assist you. Your local trade directory may give names of organizations or people offering translation services.

In all your sales promotion material make sure your message is simple and clear. The benefits to the customer of using your product should be emphasized so that he does not have to search through your literature to find out what use the product will be to him and why he should buy it from your rather than from your competitors. Too often new companies expect buyers to purchase their product because they are a wonderful company making a marvellous product, produced by the latest methods of manufacture! Interesting information but not vital information as far as the potential customer is concerned.

The message you wish to get across to customers can be communicated by any or all of the following means:

advertising in trade journals, magazines and newspapers
direct mail to companies in selected market sectors

sales leaflets for widespread distribution
sales and technical brochures
slide presentations
video presentations
articles in the trade and technical press
demonstration equipment and samples
special sales presentations

If you are making any sales or technical presentations to an audience or even to a single person always think out in advance how you should put your story across and how you are going to clinch the deal. It is easy to lose sight of the purpose of your sales presentation, namely to obtain orders. There are various ways to try and secure an order but you will be unlikely to get one unless you ask for it! This is where knowing the particular culture of a country is important since in some, such as Japan, the buyer may have to consult his colleagues before he places an order. In others such as the Middle East he may wish to argue for hours over the price. Information about the country's culture can be obtained from the DTI's *Hints to Exporters* booklets available from the country desks of the DTI, Victoria Street, London, or via your DTI regional office. The LX centres (see appendix 10) can also give advice and training on the cultural aspects as well as language tuition.

Advertising and direct mail

A small firm that sells its products by advertising or direct mail in the UK should not overlook the possibility of following the same approach in some overseas markets. European Community countries, the USA, Canada, Australia, New Zealand and South Africa are all obvious countries where you should consider such methods of selling. It is important to be aware of the legislation in each country affecting these methods of selling. Hence it is advisable to employ an advertising agent or a direct mail house who is experienced in the market. The Direct Mail Producers Association or the Direct Mail Services Standards Board can assist you to locate suitable direct mail organizations and the Chartered Institute of Marketing can give you general advice.

Sales unit

Whether or not you employ your freight forwarder or external documentary expert to look after your export or import documents it is still necessary to generate information in an appropriate form for inclusion in the documents. It is essential to have a well-organized sales office that keeps proper records and ensures that all documentary requirements are complied with correctly. In a small organization there may be only one or two people in the sales office. If there is only one person in the office then he will probably be undertaking the roles of clerk, secretary and typist. An efficient filing system is vital if you wish to maintain a close check on the progress of your business. In order to manage your sales promotion you will need to have schedules for sales visits, advertising, direct mail etc. All these need to be monitored to determine their effectiveness. For example you should use a system to identify responses from advertisements in individual magazines or journals so that you can drop those that are not effective. Your advertising agent will advise you how to do it.

If you only have a small amount of export or import business then initially the person in the sales office dealing with your UK sales can assist with your overseas work. However, if the latter becomes significant then it will be necessary to employ someone specially to handle the administration of your overseas business.

There is a triangle of basic activities in the sales and marketing function in any business. It is important to be very clear who is responsible for each activity, and yet each individual must work as part of the team and be willing to assist other members of the team when necessary. The triangle can be visualized as

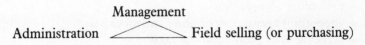

Management

Administration   Field selling (or purchasing)

When you start a business, if it is very small, you will probably do your own selling and purchasing, but very quickly you will realize the need to have someone to do one of these tasks. As the business grows there will be a need to have someone who focuses specifically on selling, i.e. visits potential agents and customers. Once you engage in international trade it is equally important to decide who will be responsible for developing your export or import business, and for meeting and dealing directly with agents and customers or suppliers, i.e. for field selling or purchasing.

When you have developed to the point where you have someone in the office and someone responsible for the field work the need for effective marketing (or purchasing) management will become more apparent. The management role is to decide the sales and marketing policies in relation to the business as a whole, to see they are implemented, to monitor progress and to take remedial action when budgets and targets are being missed.

In a small company this management role is often the responsibility of the Chief Executive or one of his fellow directors. However, unless he is a director solely concerned with the marketing and sales function he may not be able to give sufficient time to developing the overseas business.

Preparing detailed sales plans

The preparation of detailed sales plans for each market involves a great deal of work. In fact they can only be put together as you investigate each market and appoint agents, stockists and distributors or decide to sell direct to customers. The following elements generally make up the sales plan:

- choosing the markets
- selecting the sales products, packaging and labelling
- identifying the technical requirements
- evaluating competition
- appointing agents, distributors and stockists
- agreeing sales promotion methods
- establishing your sales unit and office
- organizing deliveries, documentation and insurance
- identifying costs
- establishing prices and payment terms
- determining agency sales targets and forecasts
- estimating capital requirements

The financial aspects are crucial. As an exporter or importer you must estimate the amount of capital (cash) you will require to keep you going until your business starts to make its own cash. Your accounts person should assist you to break down your annual figures. You should compare actual results with forecasts for each month and on a cumulative monthly basis as you progress through your financial year. The success or failure of your business will depend on whether or not you achieve a profitable level of sales within a reasonable time span and maintain that profitability.

Alternatives to selling from the UK

An international businessman is very much aware that there are many alternatives to the exporting or importing of goods. A manufacturer can set up a foreign subsidiary or license an overseas manufacturer to make his products. An alternative is for the producer to set up a franchising operation for the manufacture and/or sale of his products in export markets. Those in the various sectors of the service industry such as banking, tourism, health and education are also well aware of the opportunities for selling their services overseas.

Establishing a subsidiary

A possibility that is available to many SMEs is to establish a local sales branch or an assembly unit or a small manufacturing company in an overseas market, all of which are likely to involve the provision of services. Some medium-sized companies in specialized areas have deliberately developed their international business by establishing companies in overseas markets instead of supplying all markets direct from the UK. They then supply some of the manufacturing equipment and parts from the UK and receive payments, royalties and profits from the subsidiary company. Companies which already have a number of branch offices, showrooms, assembly or manufacturing units for sound reasons in different parts of the UK should seriously consider adopting the same policy approach for the single market. There are a number of factors which should cause a company to consider establishing an overseas subsidiary such as

- the need to be more responsive to local requirements
- the high cost of selling and transporting the goods relative to the manufacturing cost of the product
- potential market growth
- the need to defend an existing share of the market
- use of the overseas country as an export base to selected countries
- cheap labour and/or availability of skilled labour
- lower capital costs, e.g. cheaper land and factories
- low taxation and financial inducements

There are other factors which apply outside the single market such as tariff barriers and other obstacles to importing in the overseas market. Often the proposed introduction of new or higher barriers can lead to a rush of foreign investment as overseas suppliers seek to protect their existing business. Japanese and US companies are investing in the common market to take advantage of the changes and to overcome import barriers.

It is not always possible to establish a wholly owned subsidiary in another market because the laws of that country may restrict foreign ownership. In such circumstances it may be necessary to establish a company with a local partner or significant local participation. Unfortunately in certain countries it is not possible for the foreign company to own even a half share in the subsidiary and this can lead to many problems. Other restrictions such as limitations on the number of foreign staff that may be employed may also affect your subsidiary. In some countries an acute shortage of people with the appropriate management and technical skills can severely handicap your subsidiary. Not only may the number of work permits be limited but there may be restrictions on the number of years that you can employ a foreign national in a particular post. Furthermore, you may also be forced to have local directors who are not really committed to your business. In general small and medium-sized businesses should not consider investing in countries with these restrictions.

Assuming that you do wish to establish a subsidiary or joint venture in an overseas country, you should seek the best advice available from embassies, government agencies, banks and Chambers of Commerce as well as from professional advisers.

International accountants and international law firms based in the

UK with offices in the market are the most suitable for an SME. No positive steps should be taken to invest in an overseas market without first class professional advice and assistance. The investigations and the setting up of a foreign subsidiary will involve the full time use of the services of at least one of your directors or employees.

Licensing

Licensing is in many ways a more attractive alternative for SMEs than establishing an overseas subsidiary or joint venture. It is not an easy alternative to selling your products direct. There must be a high level of commitment from both the licenser and licensee and both parties must see and eventually realize the benefits from the licensing agreement. The benefits of licensing to the licenser are minimal investment risk, increased or new market penetration and increased returns. The licensee should also benefit from a growth in his business.

A licence is a contract whereby the owner of a product brand or manufacturing process grants the other party rights to manufacture or make use of the product, brand or process in accordance with the agreement in return for payments. The latter may be in the form of a royalty payment as well as an initial payment. Normally the licensee has to abide by certain restrictions imposed by both his own government and the licenser. A UK company can be a licensee or licenser and indeed may be both. Many UK companies benefit from the import of technical knowledge through licences such as patent licences for new inventions. Equally many UK companies benefit from licensing patents and other 'property' to overseas companies. Cross-licensing is also fairly common where different companies hold complementary patents in the same field and it is beneficial to both parties to grant a patent licence to the other.

Small firms should never lose sight of the value of patents, trademarks and registered designs. They should ensure that their intellectual property is properly registered not only in the UK but also in the single market and any other overseas markets where they wish to protect it. Nowadays it is possible to apply for a Euro-patent or a Euro-trade mark through a patent agent. Developments in Euro-legislation affecting these rights and intellectual property generally should be watched. Information on changes can be obtained from the DTI.

There are a variety of reasons for a company to adopt a licensing policy. Some of these have already been mentioned in relation to the establishment of a subsidiary or joint venture, but the following are additional reasons:

- to assist one's agent to expand his market for your products by allowing him to manufacture them
- to exploit quickly the results of any new research and development
- to overcome a lack of resources to expand manufacture at home or overseas
- to exploit a newly discovered product or process that the company itself does not wish to develop
- to counter competition in a market
- to exercise control over the manufacture and hence the availability of a quality product in a market

The licence needs to have some unique value to the licensee although it need not be exclusive especially if it is a process that can be used in several different industries. The value of a licence often does not lie solely in the information handed over at the time of the agreement – 'know how' can be equally important. The provision of training for the licensee's staff to 'show how' can be of great value to the licensee as can information on future improvements to the product or process. Any UK company thinking of importing knowledge and skills through an inward licence should also pay careful attention to these aspects of any agreement.

The choice of where and who to license and finding the right company from which to obtain a licence is often not easy. In a number of developed countries such as the USA, lists of companies with products and processes they would like to license are often published in the hope of attracting suitable interested parties. These may be of particular interest to companies in the UK looking to acquire the production know how for new processes and new products. The choice of the licensee is likely to be restricted to those companies already operating in a similar technical or commercial field and who have the necessary resources to make effective use of the licence. The licenser needs to satisfy himself that the licensee has the necessary capital, production capacity or room for new plant, and technical and commercial skills.

The licence should incorporate an on-going arrangement with the licensee so that in addition to the initial fee and royalties he will be required to pay management service and/or technical assistance fees. The licence might also incorporate the right to the licenser to inspect operations once a year to check on the quality of goods and the standard of testing.

Frequently there are government limitations on licensing. The licenser may find that his 'property' is technically sensitive for defence and other reasons and therefore he may not be able to license it without his government's approval. The licensee's government may place a number of restrictions on the licensee. If it is for the manufacture of a product then the parties may have to agree that a minimum percentage of the production be exported. There may be restrictions on the repatriation of fees and royalties such as taxes to be paid before they can be transferred. Problems may also arise if payments have to be made in a hard currency and the country is short of such currencies. This is the situation in many developing countries.

Instead of taking the whole of the initial fee or the full percentage royalty payments, the licenser may decide to accept a share of the equity of the licensee. Thus the licenser becomes entitled to dividends and any capital appreciation. In addition he may be able to negotiate for a seat on the board of the licensee. It may also be desirable to have the right to convert royalties into equity.

It is common practice for the licenser to place conditions and restrictions on the licensee relating to the following:

use of alternative trade names
marketing areas including exporting
supply sources for capital equipment, parts and raw materials
improvements in the product or process made by the licensee

Usually the licensee must advise the licenser of any improvements or changes made to the product or process. The licenser should also establish the right to use these improvements and any patentable 'property' in his own business. If the licensee, through his own research and development, acquires patented knowledge then the licenser should not only have the right to a licence but also have it free of charge or for a normal commercial fee. The contract between both parties must cover the transfer of any patents, trademarks, copyright, designs whether registered or not and any other information relevant to the 'property' being licensed.

Overseas staffing

Whether you are engaging in a joint venture, a licensing operation or the setting up of a subsidiary, it is likely that at some point you will have to send someone overseas to work with your contract partner for a period. This is likely to be anything from three years upwards especially if a new plant is being built based on your designs and know how.

Considerable care needs to be taken in selecting someone to go and live overseas for a period. If the person is married and has children then there may be additional problems and expense if the children are at a critical age for schooling. The husband and wife must both be capable of adapting to living in a different environment, possibly one with a different language, culture and religion to their own.

It is important to ensure that people being sent overseas on secondment are given sufficient training in the language and culture of the overseas country before they depart so that they can adapt quickly to the new circumstances. The LX centres, the School of Oriental and African Studies in London University and the Centre for International Briefing, Farnham, can all provide appropriate training and briefing. A non-profit-making organization known as Employment Conditions Abroad Ltd provides a unique information and advisory service on the terms and conditions of employment for staff working in an overseas country.

Franchising

Franchising is of interest both to those who want to export unique knowledge and skills and those who wish to import them. In this type of operation the franchisee generally uses the name of the franchiser. The latter licenses the franchisee to produce, pack, distribute and sell his product in return for a fee which is probably an annual fee. Usually far more is involved than just a licensing agreement. In a good franchising operation the franchisee will receive training, a detailed package of how to set up and sell the product, a measure of continuous control over his operations to see he maintains standards and updating on any improvements and changes. A successful franchise operation involves a good initial package, and a back-up of service which does not only involve the supply of raw materials. All these points should be covered in a legal contract which should clearly define the rights and obligations of the franchiser and franchisee.

Franchising operations are now well established in the high streets of many countries and cover a wide range of relationships. Typical franchising involves products and services such as

fast foods
oil and petrol
public houses and hotels
car dealers
bottling of products with high water content, e.g. soft drinks
brand name textiles

Although many of these franchise business areas have been established over many years and the franchisers have sound reputations and good track records over a long period, nevertheless before entering into a franchising operation a number of points must be considered such as the following.

- Will the franchisee require any special skills or previous experience?
- Will help and advice be available to the franchisee when needed?
- How readily will finance be available to the franchisee?
- Will the franchiser be able to give credible support to the franchisee for the obtaining of finance or can he help arrange finance for the franchisee?
- Are all reasonable steps being taken to ensure the franchisee does not become one of the business failures?
- Is training and assistance provided to the franchisee immediately he signs the agreement?
- Will the franchiser's purchasing power, e.g. for bulk raw materials, really assist the franchisee?
- How will the franchisee pay the franchiser, e.g. by paying a start up fee and fees for services, by a commission on sales or from the mark up on goods supplied?

- Will the franchiser and franchisee be able to keep pace with changes in the market place?
- Will the franchisee be able to operate the working hours required, which are likely to be especially long in the beginning?
- How will the franchiser and franchisee maintain high standards of quality and service?
- Will the franchisee accept the controls imposed by the franchiser?
- Will the franchisee be operating in the right location and be free from serious competition?
- Is the franchiser able to give the franchisee the necessary national support through advertising and other forms of promotion?

All these considerations are even more relevant when the franchiser and the franchisee are in different countries. Small firms should always look at the possibility of being a franchiser as an option for developing their business if they have a unique product or service. Similarly if they are in certain business sectors in the UK they should consider from whom they might obtain a franchise for a product or service in order to expand their business. In view of the widespread interest in franchising there are now exhibitions, conferences and seminars on the subject. Anyone contemplating becoming involved in franchise operations should attend an exhibition to learn about the industry and a suitable seminar to learn how to do it. Information can also be obtained from the British Franchise Association Ltd.

Key points

- Make sure that you are aware of the various methods of selling in an overseas market.
- If you are intending to use them choose agents and distributors with care – they are your link with the market.
- Consider the possibility of selling your products or services direct to customers.
- Sales promotion is vital – make sure that you are sending the right signals to your market.
- Agree accurate sales forecasts with your agents if you are exporting, and standards of quality and service from the suppliers if you are importing.
- Don't establish a subsidiary without consulting local agencies as well as your professional advisers.
- Licensing can be attractive – but be careful when drawing up contracts that you are not restricting your future activities unduly.
- Franchising will demand more commitments on your part – make sure that you fully understand the agreements you are entering into.

4

International trade and payment

Outline

Ensuring that you are paid promptly and in full is the key to international trade. This chapter explains:

- credit assessment
- credit insurance
- the role of the Export Credits Guarantee Department
- contractual terms for payment
- giving credit
- currency exchange rate risk
- guarantees and bonds
- sales conditions
- counter-trade
- importing
- consignment stocks
- factoring

Ensuring safe payment

The most important part of completing any sale is to ensure as far as is possible that you will receive payment for your goods on time. A customer in Europe may wish to buy ex works in sterling especially if he has his own transport coming to the UK, or he may wish to buy after delivery to his warehouse and pay in his local currency. He may be willing to pay in advance of receipt of the goods or at sight, i.e. on taking physical possession of the goods, or he may want credit. Your payment terms must take the customer's requirements into consideration but they need not and probably should not be better than those offered by competitors. Trying to beat competition by offering more attractive payment terms can be a very expensive exercise.

Credit assessment

It is prudent to check on the credit worthiness of any potential agent or customer before you engage in transactions. Naturally you should also always be alert to any deterioration in his financial status. The first indication of a change is usually when the client begins to pay you more slowly!

There are many organizations in the developed countries that will provide, for a fee, information on the credit worthiness of a company. Dunn & Bradstreet Ltd are one of the best-known multinational companies in this field. They also offer business information, direct mail and debt collecting services. Another UK company in this field is CCN Systems Ltd who provide a full range of business and credit information on any company in Europe. They can be contacted direct or accessed via the Europe Network Ltd database. Also Graydon-ATP International Ltd provide international credit reports on companies in over 160 countries. Your clearing bank may also be able to obtain credit status information on your potential agent or customer.

The only alternative to checking on the credit worthiness of your customers is to sell using guaranteed payment terms. Should a customer appear to becoming financially insecure then you should always insist on guaranteed payment terms such as payment in advance before making further deliveries.

Credit insurance

The purpose of credit insurance is to protect the seller against a payment default by the buyer, or in the case of the ECGD, political or economic 'default' by the buyer's country preventing payment being made. Normally it is not possible for a small firm to insure the credit risk alone until their annual export turnover reaches a reasonable level, e.g. £100,000 per annum. However, by linking the credit risk to export financing it is possible for firms with smaller turnover to obtain cover, e.g. through bank short-term export finance such as the 'Smaller Exports Schemes' run by Barclays Bank plc.

The Export Credits Guarantee Department

The Export Credits Guarantee Department (ECGD) is a department of government responsible to the DTI. It has two main classes of business:

i) Comprehensive credit insurance for repetition trade. There is a variety of schemes available through the ECGD for small firms whose export turnover is in excess of £100,000 per annum (although realistically, firms will probably be turning over not less than £250,000 per annum) and who will be able to maintain their own ECGD policy. The main one, the ECGD comprehensive short-term guarantee policy, is for goods sold on up to six month's credit. Normally, the policy will cover a company's turnover, and will pay out up to 95 per cent of the value of exports where the buyer does not pay. Where desired, the comprehensive short-term policy can be assigned in whole or in part to a bank or other financing organizations to obtain export finance.

ii) Guarantees for the financing of special capital goods and project contracts. These guarantees will be agreed between the ECGD and the seller. They are very specialized and advice should be taken as to the types of agreements covered.

The international services branch of your bank should be able to advise you on all ECGD policies. Alternatively, you can try contacting the ECGD direct. They will be pleased to advise you or provide a booklet covering their services.

Other credit insurance

There is a growing private market in export credit insurance for firms whose total export turnover is sufficiently high to be attractive to the insurers. Organizations such as CAD Consultants Limited and Unicol Export Insurance Services Limited offer a comprehensive service on credit management as well as export credit insurance. Finance facilities are also available as a separate part of the service package should they be required. Although the overall package cost for the schemes may be too expensive for a small firm that is just starting to export, nonetheless, they should investigate them and perhaps start with a selection of the services.

One way a small firm can look for export credit insurance is by contacting the British Insurance Brokers Association (BIBA) for the names of suitable brokers. As the large brokers have regional offices, there should be no difficulty in finding one within reasonable distance of your premises.

Credit insurance can be used to help obtain finance, either by assignment of a credit insurance policy or under a bank export finance scheme. Since credit insurance is often tied to financing, it is important to be clear about what you need for your business. If you do not require credit insurance, there are many other possibilities for financing which the local international service branch of your bank will be able to discuss with you.

Contractual terms for payment

In many countries in Europe and North America and even in Japan customers in certain sectors such as big departmental stores will agree to pay in advance either a deposit or the full invoice value.

Cash payment

The simplest method of payment is to ask for cash before you despatch the goods or even before you make them. Asking for COD, i.e. the carrier hands over the goods on receipt of payment, is only effective in countries with no exchange problems and no restrictions (as in the USA). Unfortunately there may be considerable delays before you receive payment from some countries because of exchange control procedures.

Should you be selling in packages below 20 kg in weight and within the accepted dimensions then you could sell via the Royal Mail Parcel Post on cash on delivery (COD) terms. Express freight companies in Europe and North America will also collect payments for you but they are usually more expensive than the Royal Mail Parcels Service. It may take some time for money to reach you when you sell on COD terms – especially from certain countries.

Open account trading

The advent of the single market means that in Europe companies will be obliged by the effects of competition and pressure from buyers to sell on the same payment terms as local suppliers, i.e. on open account. This simply means that whenever you despatch goods you send the buyer an invoice, usually for payment at the end of each month. The buyer will send you a cheque or banker's draft in sterling or local currency, or he can arrange a money transfer through the bank using telegraphic transfer or an international money order. This method carries the same degree of payment risk as in the UK with the additional problem that it may be more difficult and more costly to visit the overseas customer to chase him for payment – unless his offices are just the other side of the Channel Tunnel!

Documentary collections

The documentary collection system of payment involves sending all the documents relating to the sale and shipment of the goods via the seller's bank to the buyer's bank. This includes not only the invoice stating the payment method but all the shipping documents. The buyer's bank notifies the buyer when they have the documents and the buyer will then pay at sight or accept a bill of exchange (see Glossary), i.e. a bill that allows the buyer credit. Usually bills of exchange (see appendix 19) are drawn by the seller on the overseas buyer and the latter must sign his acceptance on the bill before he can obtain the documents and title to the goods. There are various terms used for immediate payment such as 'cash against documents', 'documents against payment', 'payment at sight' and, for term bills, 'documents against acceptance'.

Blank bills of exchange can be bought from your local bank or law stationers or from Croner Publications Ltd or Tate Freight Forms. The seller completes the details as if it is a type of cheque, if necessary with the help of his bank. The bill of exchange is then passed by his bank to the seller's bank with the other documents at the time of despatch of the goods. A bill of lading or airway bill must be included with these documents. The bill of lading or a similar document is evidence of despatch. The goods should not be despatched direct to the buyer – otherwise you have lost title to the goods before the buyer has agreed to pay. Your freight forwarder and your agent or the buyer will advise you where you need to send them to await release.

Letters of credit (LC)

A documentary LC is a written undertaking given by the buyer's bank to pay the seller the sum shown upon the seller's performing in accordance with the description, terms and conditions laid down in the LC and agreed between the parties. There are a number of types of LC but the main differences are between revocable and irrevocable LCs and between confirmed and unconfirmed LCs. A revocable LC is one which can be revoked, one which the *buyer* can cancel. It would be most unwise to accept one as it is not a guarantee of payment since the buyer can revoke it at any time. Irrevocable LCs, on the other hand, bind the buyer from the moment of issue.

Normally payment under an LC will depend on the issuing bank's undertaking to pay monies due. With a confirmed irrevocable LC, the confirming bank, usually a bank in the seller's country will guarantee payment under the LC, once the seller has fulfilled its terms. Normally the seller will stipulate the confirming bank, but the buyer pays the confirming fees as well as all the other fees in his own country for opening the LC. If the buyer is not able to pay the confirming fees it may be sensible for the seller to pay them to be sure of receiving payment.

There are various types of special LCs such as revolving and transferable LCs and your bank will explain the meaning should you receive one.

Although LCs are regarded as the safest method of payment, to obtain this benefit the seller must comply exactly with the terms of the LC. Unfortunately many companies find it very difficult to provide all documents and act exactly as required. When this happens there are often long delays before documents can be corrected and the money collected from the bank. In some cases companies have never been able to obtain payment.

Always ask your bank to check on the validity of an LC as

unfortunately there are a number of fraudulent LCs being sent to overseas suppliers from less scrupulous buyers in certain countries. In negotiating an LC the parties will have to agree the following points:

price and delivery terms
latest date for shipment
description of the goods
method of payment, place of payment and currency
method of shipment, i.e. air, road or sea with or without trans-shipment and whether or not part shipments are allowed
documents required by the buyer such as certificates of origin, quality certificates, import licences, invoice etc.
name of bank opening the LC
responsibility for bank charges

These must be agreed in advance because the buyer will need to stipulate them to his bank when he opens the LC. The buyer normally requires a pro forma invoice in order to be able to obtain an LC from his bank. A pro forma invoice is a normal invoice but with the words 'pro forma' written on it. Your actual invoice goes with the documents which you present with the LC when you want payment.

Should you receive an LC which contains any terms and conditions with which you are unable to comply you should immediately telephone, telex or fax your buyer asking him to authorize his bank to issue an amendment. Do not despatch your goods until you have the amendment.

Naturally if you are selling to your agent or to a customer whom you know you can trust you can 'ship on trust' knowing the buyer will issue through his bank the required amendments to the LC.

SITPRO, a UK government organization, issue a 'Letter of Credit Checklist and Guide for Export Sales Executives'. This is of invaluable help to any company expecting to be involved in LC payments.

LCs, like bills of exchange, can be for payment at sight when shipment has been made or at 30, 60, 90, 180 or 360 days from the date of the bill of lading or other documentary proof of the date of shipment.

Giving credit

If you do give credit, this can be done in two ways depending on whether your payment is to be by documentary or non-documentary methods.

Where a payment is to be by non-documentary methods, e.g. open account, credit terms can be arranged in the same way as in the UK. The contract should stipulate that payment should take place within a certain time after invoicing.

Where payment is to be by documentary methods, the normal way of giving credit is by way of a 'term' bill of exchange.

Term bills call for payment 30, 60, 90 or even 180 days after sight or after date of shipment, e.g. date of bill of lading. It is fairly common practice in Europe for sellers to ask the buyer's bank to avalise bills of exchange. This means in effect that the buyer's bank guarantees payment. However, if the bill is not avalised and the buyer fails to pay the bill at maturity, you can ask your bank to 'protest' the bill as being unpaid with the seller's bank. The overseas bank will be required to instruct a notary public, who in turn will require the buyer to state the reason for non-payment on a 'deed of protest'. This together with the dishonoured bill is the basis for any legal action for damages etc. If the bill remains unpaid you can ask your agent, your freight forwarder or the bank to arrange for the return of the goods, to release them to someone else such as your agent or another buyer or to put them up for auction. In the meantime you will have been incurring additional demurrage (warehousing) and insurance charges. Clearly you need to be confident of your customer's credit worthiness and reliability before allowing him to pay by means of a term bill. However, it is safer than open account trading. The ICC issues a code of practice for drafts or bills of exchange entitled *Uniform Rules for Collections* – it will help you to settle any disputes.

Financing your exports

It is often difficult for a small firm to finance the development of its export business especially if it is necessary to grant credit terms to agents and direct customers. One possibility is to seek additional capital, bank finance for instance. However, there are also a variety of methods of obtaining early 'payment' against a shipment; these are known as post-shipment financing. In the first instance you should discuss your requirements with the bank. They will suggest ways of raising extra finance.

Selling bills

It is possible to sell bills of exchange with or without recourse. The amount you receive will depend on the standing of the customer, the customer's bank and country. If any of them are of poor standing you will receive very little for your bill and you will obtain less if you sell without recourse. Banks will make advances of money against good bills of exchange or confirmed irrevocable LCs. If 'payment' for the transaction is required before all the documents are available, then the bank will 'negotiate' an advance. If the supporting documents are complete such as with a 180-day bill or LC then the bank will provide advances by 'discounting' your bill of exchange or LC. If there is a default in payment then the bank may or may not have recourse to you for the money they have advanced. This will depend on who is responsible for the default.

Making and receiving payment

An international trader can remit and receive funds in a variety of ways.

Cheque	This may appear to be simple but you need to know that the cheque will be met when it is presented and that it will be in a freely transferable currency, i.e. you can exchange the foreign currency for sterling without any difficulty except for the exchange rate risk
Banker's draft	The buyer arranges with his bank to issue a draft drawn in either sterling or a foreign currency. Payment is assured when this is paid into the seller's bank account. You may wish to open some foreign currency accounts at

	your own bank if you can use foreign currency for your own overseas purchases
Telegraphic transfer	This avoids many of the banking system delays arising from other methods of payment and is the quickest way to transfer funds from the buyer's to the seller's bank using telecommunications. The seller should be aware that he has to ask the buyer to pay by telegraphic transfer. The buyer will then instruct his bank to pay from his account by this method
International payment order	The buyer's bank will use a courier or air mail services to instruct a bank in the seller's country, or elsewhere if required, to pay the seller. The latter should state where he wishes to be paid
International money order	This is a very good way for buyers paying for small amounts. Sellers should ask for sterling orders unless they have a use for other hard currencies. The buyer obtains the money order from his own bank and sends it to the seller. Payment is assured when the seller pays it into his account

To be a successful international trader you need to acquire knowledge and develop skills with regard to pricing, methods of payment and financing. All this you will acquire by learning and by experience. Initially a small firm should avoid complex methods of payment and keep any financing and risks to the minimum. It is important, however, to be aware of the various methods of payment and financing since, as your export business expands to new countries, sooner or later a buyer will propose a new payment arrangement.

Currency exchange rate risk

Any company which engages in international trade will sooner or later have to receive or pay in a foreign currency. It is essential to transact business only in currencies which are freely transferable, otherwise known as hard currencies. All the Common Market countries have hard currencies and most are freely transferable now or will be after 1992 when any licensing or other restrictions will have been removed. Unfortunately exchange rates even between hard currencies such as sterling and the dollar can fluctuate quite significantly over a period of a few months. This can have a serious effect on your competitiveness and on your profit. There are several ways of reducing or eliminating this risk, and it is important to discuss with your bank how you can protect your profit margin in sterling when you are receiving or paying out in another currency.

Guarantees and Bonds

A guarantee is an assurance made through a third party, such as a bank, that if the contract is not performed according to its terms, the bank will pay the beneficiary a sum of money. Guarantees can cover contractual compliance, for example agreement to pay for goods, or they can cover physical performance, for example a contract to build a bridge. Guarantees are sometimes referred to as bonds.

A guarantee will cover, for example, 10 per cent of the value of the goods or services being provided. It would generally be required by buyers in certain countries in connection with contracts to supply government agencies.

Guarantees can be conditional on proof of non performance. Normally, however, they will be 'unconditional' and payment will be made on first demand by the buyer. For this reason, you should try to avoid simple 'demand' guarantees since these mean that the bank will pay on the first demand of the buyer. You are at the mercy of the buyer since, if he claims, the bank will require you to repay any money paid out under the guarantee. It is most important to clarify under what circumstances the buyer can claim under the guarantee, to have a closing date when it will cease to be valid and to specify who can claim under the guarantee, e.g. not third parties. A guarantee may be arranged to become effective once the contract is accepted. It indicates your ability to act in accordance with the contract. Your bank will charge you a fee for issuing the guarantee.

Guarantees have caused many problems for both the sellers and the banks. ICC (UK) with other ICC bodies overseas plan to publish a code of practice on guarantees.

Apart from the ordinary guarantees mentioned above there are many other types of guarantee and any company involved in offering a guarantee or performance bond should consult their independent professional advisers or the local international services branch of their bank.

Sales conditions

Whether you are an exporter or an importer you should have a standard set of sales terms and conditions (see appendix 1) which are printed on the back of your quotation forms, and sometimes on the back of or attached to your invoice or sales contract. If the conditions are on the back of your sales contract, state in your quotation that they are included in the contract to ensure that they form part of it. Similarly when acknowledging orders always refer to your sales conditions. A useful checklist of terms and conditions of sale is published by the Chemical Industries Association. Any or all of the following subjects should be included in clauses in the terms and conditions. Examples are given of what might appear under each heading.

Price	Duration and variability
Quantity	Tolerances
Quality	Fitness for what purposes and specifications
Warranties and liabilities	Liability limitations, time limit on claims
Delivery	Any special conditions or requirements
Packaging, containers etc.	Special provisions, e.g. return of containers
Payment	Interest on overdue accounts
Default by buyer	Right to cancel the contract
Risk and property	When risk passes from seller to buyer
Force majeure	Strikes, wars, government interference that frustrate the contract
Assignment	Seller's right to sell – contraction or assignment of benefits
Insurance	Any special needs
Incoterms	Statement that 'Incoterms 1980' or 'Incoterms 1990' apply

Diversion of goods	Seller's right to divert
Arbitration	Who will arbitrate in disputes
Law	Specification that English law applies
Jurisdiction	Specification of UK arbitration or English Courts

A sample set of sales conditions appears in appendix 1. It is essential, however, that you discuss your requirements with an international lawyer. In addition you should discuss your sales conditions with your agent, distributor or stockist as they will need to apply similar conditions when reselling any of your goods.

Should you send a confirmation of the receipt of an order then this should include the following to avoid misunderstandings:

names and addresses of buyer and seller
product details including packing information
method of transport
payment and delivery terms
value of the order including any agreed charges
delivery promise or indication
standard terms and conditions of sale
any other details agreed between buyer and seller

The same details should appear on the invoice.

Counter-trade

One of the commonest forms of counter-trade is barter where there is straightforward exchange of goods. This is a method not infrequently used by Eastern European countries and other countries short of hard currencies. Vienna used to be the centre for counter-trading especially with Eastern Europe but today traders in London probably arrange more counter-trade business. The DTI can provide a list of London-based counter-traders and you should not enter into any deal of this nature without having a counter-trade expert to assist you.

It is quite common in some countries for buyers to ask you to accept post payment in goods especially if they and their country are short of hard currency. In general you should not attempt to resell any goods directly yourself unless you can find a merchant or retailer who will buy the goods from you at an agreed price. It is better to find a merchant in London or Vienna who is used to such deals and will agree a price and specification for the goods. Thus you will know the effects on your profit and the increased prices you need to quote before you enter into the deal. The merchant or factor who takes the buyer's goods and pays you will normally look for a commission of 10–20 per cent.

Importing

The various methods of payment apply equally to importers although naturally they should seek the best terms they can obtain from the exporters. In general unless you are confident in your supplier and there are sound reasons for doing so you should not pay the full amount for your goods in advance. From the buyer's point of view it is an advantage if you do not have to pay until you receive title to the goods and preferably not until you physically possess them and have been able to inspect them. The more you can reassure your supplier of your credit worthiness, the better the payment terms you are likely to secure. Equally you should satisfy yourself that your supplier has the financial and other resources to meet your requirements.

Consignment stocks

If you are trading in goods yourself on the basis of sale or return then you may wish to persuade your overseas supplier to supply you with goods on consignment. This means that you take the imported goods into your stock but you do not pay for them until you have sold or used them. Until the goods are sold they remain the property of the overseas buyer but you are responsible for their safe keeping. As the importer you should agree with the buyer who pays for their insurance and for loss, damage or theft. You should keep careful records of all goods received, held in stock and sold, checking physically from time to time that your records agree with the actual stocks. In order to avoid any arguments it is essential to agree that if the goods have not been sold after a certain period, e.g. three or six months, then either the goods will be paid for or returned.

Consignment stocks require a great deal of trust between the buyer and seller and both must follow sound business practices if problems are to be avoided. Manufacturers purchasing parts or other materials might think this a good way to reduce their stock costs. It does lead to administrative complications and they would be wisest to consider instead having a 'just in time' delivery service.

Factoring

There are a number of companies in the UK, some closely involved with the banks, who offer a factoring service. They should be members of the Association of British Factors from whom you can obtain a list of factoring companies that might meet your requirements. In general factors are looking for customers with an export turnover of not less than £100,000 per annum and who are growing rapidly.

Factors provide exporters with integrated services, sales accounting and collection of payments, credit management with credit insurance if required and advances of money against invoices. They assume total responsibility for these functions including asses ing the credit worthiness of customers. If it is non-recourse factoring (i.e. no claims upon the suppliers for repayment) then the factor gives full protection against all the bad debts on approved sales.

A small firm should seriously consider factoring since it will save them administrative costs and management time and provide them with a guaranteed cash flow. It will release resources for further expansion of their business. Businesses using factoring include those in manufacturing, distribution, the service sector, transport and construction. It is mainly used by those in the first three areas of activity. Factors will cover UK as well as export sales and handle invoices and payments in all hard currencies. If your home sales are substantial and your export sales are small but growing, look for a factor who will accept all your business.

Key points

- Consult your professional advisers to establish the most appropriate terms and methods of payment.
- Be sure to check the credit worthiness of overseas customers.
- There are many sources of information — be sure to gather as much relevant data and advice as you can before making important decisions.

5

Delivering the product

Outline

Success in exporting depends upon getting the product to the customer on time and in good condition. This chapter analyses:

- delivery terms
- different modes of transport including road, rail, sea and air
- insurance
- packaging and labelling
- customs practice
- documentation
- parcel post

The delivery of goods to customers in overseas markets requires the same care and attention to detail as is needed in the UK. Some aspects of moving the goods from one country to another can look very daunting to the newcomer to international trade. However, there are many organizations engaged in freight forwarding and in the transport field who are ready and willing to assist you. The Institute of Freight Forwarders should be one of your first points of contact. For example, they will provide you with lists of freight forwarders who can arrange the documentation and movement of goods to those parts of the world to which you wish to export. If you describe the type of goods you wish to move and where you want them sent they will select freight forwarders who have the knowledge and experience to act for you. However, it is important to acquire a sufficient understanding of all aspects of moving goods so as to be able to discuss with your freight forwarder delivery times, modes of transport, packing, labelling and documentation.

Delivery terms

Delivery terms are an important part of your price quotation; they also affect your costs quite significantly and all international traders should be fully aware of the use and obligations of any delivery term. These have been incorporated into a generally accepted international code by the ICC under the title 'Incoterms'. They are varied from time to time – Incoterms 1990 are a revision of Incoterms 1980. The 1990 code rearranges the terms according to a new system and introduces some new alpha codes.

The order of the terms in the 1990 codes are as follows: EXW, FCA, FAS, FOB, CFR, CIF, CPT, CIP, DAF, DES, DEQ, DUU/DPP. Detailed information on these terms can be obtained direct from ICC in London. However, the main terms in use have the following meanings:

Ex Works (EXW)   The buyer arranges for the collection and loading of the goods at the supplier's premises. The buyer has title to the goods at the time of loading. The seller must pack and label the goods and have them ready for collection at the time and place stipulated in the sales contract. The buyer needs to insure the goods from the point at which they are loaded and include cover for damage during loading.

Free Carrier (FCA)   This term should be used instead of FOB when through road transport is used and includes using roll on and roll off (RO/RO) ferries. It should also be used for container shipments where different types of transport are utilized on a door to door basis rather than port to port. The goods pass to the buyer at the time and place (destination) stipulated in the sales contract, e.g. inland depot. The seller must notify the buyer by rapid communication when the goods are handed over to the carrier in accordance with the buyer's instructions. The seller retains the title and risk in the goods until the carrier receives them, at which point the buyer takes the title and risk.

Free on Board (FOB)   The seller packs and delivers the goods on board a vessel at a UK or European port. The buyer may stipulate which vessel or line is to be used and the port of loading. The seller is responsible for all costs and risks until the goods have passed over the ship's rail, and must notify the buyer with the shipping information when the goods are on board.

Cost and Freight (CFR) This term used to be known as C and F. The seller packs and labels the goods for export and arranges for the goods to be shipped to a named port of destination and unloaded. The seller must obtain any export licence and the buyer any import licence that may be required. The goods must be despatched in the period stipulated in the sales contract and the seller must insure until the goods have at least passed over the ship's rail, when the risk passes to the buyer. The seller must obtain a clear negotiable bill of lading for the buyer.

Cost Insurance and Freight (CIF) In addition to the obligations which are the same as under CFR the seller must have a marine insurance policy to cover risks in transit. The policy should cover the CIF price plus 10 per cent and if possible be in the same currency as the sales contract. Buyers should normally insist on an 'all risk' type of policy.

Freight Carriage Paid (CPT) This should be used when road transport (including RO/RO) or multi-modal transport is employed. The seller arranges and pays transport to the destination point and obtains any necessary export licence. The seller is responsible for any risks to the goods until the first carrier takes them over when the risk passes to the buyer. The buyer is also responsible for any import licences and customs duties. The seller must notify the buyer by telephone, fax or telex as soon as he has passed the goods to the first carrier.

Freight Carriage and Insurance Paid (CIP) This is used when road transport (including RO/RO) or multi-modal transport is employed. It carries the same obligation as a CPT quotation with the addition that the seller must take out insurance under which the buyer is also entitled to claim. The seller must advise the buyer of the nature of the cover if he wishes to take out additional insurance.

Delivered Duty Unpaid (DDU) or Delivered Duty Paid (DDP) This is used irrespective of the mode of transport and the seller bears all the costs, including the insurance, of getting the goods to an agreed destination point on the date specified. He must obtain export and import licences and pay all charges at the destination and see that the buyer is advised immediately the goods are placed with the first carrier. Duties will be paid either by the buyer (DDU) or by the seller (DDP).

Other Incoterms used less often are as follows.

Free Alongside Ship (FAS)   The seller delivers goods alongside the ship. The buyer must arrange clearance for export, loading, transport, insurance and import clearance.

Delivered at Frontier (DAF)   This is used for road and multi-modal transport. The seller is responsible for the goods until they reach the frontier of the destination country.

Ex Ship (EXS)   The seller is responsible for the goods until they are unloaded at the destination port.

Ex Quay (EXQ)   The seller is responsible until they leave the quay at the point of destination and hence he may be responsible for customs clearance.

It is important to note the changes in the 1990 Incoterms in comparison with the 1980 terms. The alpha code changes are:

1980	*1990*
DCP	CDT
EXS	DES
EXQ	DEQ
DDP alone	DDP/DDU
FOP/FOT and FOA	FCA

Until everyone is familiar with the 1990 terms and they have all been accepted worldwide as well as by the UK the quotation should indicate which Incoterms are being used, e.g. CDT Incoterms 1990 or DCP Incoterms 1980.

A typical seller's quotation might be

'Product name' £10 per kilo FOB UK Port (Incoterms 1990)

Transport modes

Detailed information on the different methods of transport can be found with other useful information in the professional guide of the Institute of Freight Forwarders, *Exporter and Forwarder*, which is published in the Spring every year. Handling freight and all the associated documentation can be complicated. If a small firm feels it is going to be too difficult for them they should ask a freight forwarder to handle everything. However, it is advantageous to have some understanding of the international transport market.

International road haulage

The rapid growth in road transport throughout continental Europe and beyond, into the Middle East and North Africa, has occurred in the last 30 years. It has provided exporters with undreamt-of means of moving their goods securely and speedily to their customers. The RO/RO ferries have enabled fairly short sea crossings to be undertaken without any serious hold ups.

There are two types of international haulage – driver-accompanied operations and unaccompanied operations. In the former operation the driver, perhaps with an assistant driver, remains with the vehicle from the point of loading to the point of unloading. On long distances the drivers will take it in turns to drive and rest or sleep or they will stop the night at special vehicle parks.

The unaccompanied service is one where a tractor unit and driver haul a loaded trailer from the loading point to the point of shipment. The trailer is left on board a ferry or loaded separately by the port employees. The trailer travels unaccompanied to the port of destination. If the trailer is to travel a very long distance it may have many changes of driver and tractor unit during the journey.

Unaccompanied services are generally cheaper than accompanied services but less secure. Goods may suffer damage while the trailer is being moved between transport modes, or pilferage may occur where the trailer is unaccompanied, so the choice of service you make is an important decision.

International rail haulage

The creation of the internal market has given a major impetus to the improvement in rail freight services throughout the countries involved. The opening of the Channel Tunnel in 1993 should give a further impetus to the benefit of all exporters. Currently British Rail's Railfreight Distribution Services are timed to connect with the continental railways' network of express freight trains. These are known as TEEM (Trans Europe Express Merchandise). Intercontainer, the marketing arm of participating continental railways including Eastern block countries, moves containers through a network of dedicated trains. (Contact Railfreight Distribution at 169 Westbourne Terrace, London W2 6JY, tel: 01–922 6737.)

Red Star Express Parcels: although there is now a worldwide service for sending parcels express by air to many countries, within Europe there is the Eurail Express system which links with the Red Star Europe. The latter are responsible for final delivery or collection by road unless the Red Star–Eurail parcel points are used at the stations.

Shipping

The shipping market divides roughly into ferry services like those between the UK and Europe and vessels on intercontinental routes outside Europe. Most of the latter are served by conference lines and independent lines.

Conference lines provide a regular service on a standard route. The conference is composed of a group of shipping lines with the same conditions of operation and rates. The independent lines operate outside the conference lines arrangements and may not provide the same regularity of service. Their rates are generally lower than those of the conference lines.

Many of the shipping routes now use container ships which improves security and leads to faster turnrounds in the ports. It is important to distinguish between FCL (full container load) and LCL (less than full container load). An FCL implies that it contains only one supplier's products. Normally an FCL will go from your warehouse direct to your agent's or customer's premises.

An LCL contains several suppliers' products. These have to be grouped together at the freight carrier's depot for despatch and separated again at a depot in the receiving country. This groupage operation leads to delays and a considerable increase in the risk of losing goods through theft and damage, especially in certain countries. You should discuss with your freight forwarder the best way of moving your goods.

Air freight

Air freight now plays a very important role in the export of goods from the UK accounting for approximately 15 per cent of UK exports by value. These are mainly high value goods or those that are required very urgently such as spare parts. However, there are certain parts of the world such as Central Africa which are still very difficult to reach in a reasonable time other than by air. In addition if you are sending goods half-way round the world, e.g. to Hong Kong, you may find some worthwhile savings by using air freight instead of sea freight. Two or three days' delivery means that you and your customer can carry lower stocks, and you reduce transit risks. You should also be able to receive payment more quickly by reducing your credit terms if they are based on date of despatch, or because they arrive speedily if they are based on the date of arrival.

Air freight rates are usually higher than sea freight rates. Your freight forwarder should always alert you to special low air freight rates to countries with high exports and low imports by air. In these circumstances the airlines are very keen to fill the empty space for the return journey.

Courier and express services

Over the past few years there has been a rapid expansion in courier and express freight services. Courier services provide for the goods to be accompanied or carried by hand so that they reach their destination within a specified period. The main use of courier services has been for the rapid movement of vital documents or small highly valued goods. The service for documents is likely to decline as greater use is made of fax and other electronic systems for transmitting information and documents.

Express freight services have grown very rapidly in Europe and North America and usually goods can be moved from the point of departure to the point of delivery within 24 or 48 hours. Some companies are now quoting varying rates according to the specified period of delivery. Additional services are provided by some of the express freight companies such as an export document service and a payment collection service. If you wish you can deal direct with these express freight services because they will do the same work for you as a freight forwarder would do with respect to the business placed. Rates for express services are usually higher than for normal freight services; in addition there are limitations on the weight and size of parcels. If you do not need a 24- or 48-hour delivery the Royal Mail Parcels Service should be considered. Particularly in Europe parcels will generally be delivered in a few days and their rates are lower than others. Most small firms should consider the Royal Mail Parcels Service first when choosing a parcels service.

Insurance

The need to keep risks to the minimum is paramount in any small firm. However, as in larger companies it is necessary to weigh up the risks of doing any particular piece of business against the cost of protection. Insurance plays an important part in all overseas business for every company whether they are a supplier of goods or of services. You need to consider insurance for your goods against loss or damage and for your payments against the customer's failure to pay and against any other risk such as product liability. Since insurance is a complex area a small firm should always use a registered insurance broker to advise them and to find the best policies for their company's business.

The agents and services your company uses should themselves always have adequate insurance.

Fortunately, a freight forwarder who is a trading member of the Institute of Freight Forwarders, for instance, must have appropriate and sufficient cover.

Cargo insurance

Cargo insurance is a must for all exporters and importers at least up to the time the title to the goods passes to your customer or from when the title passes to you from the supplier. A certificate of insurance is a necessary part of the documentation for an exporter shipping under a Cost, insurance and freight (CIF) contract. You should insure for the value of the goods plus 10 per cent, or more specifically CIF value plus 10 per cent to cover, for example, chasing and handling costs should the goods have to be moved to a store for inspection at the destination point. Sometimes exporters prefer to insure their goods up to the point where the customer takes physical possession of the goods. This is in case he rejects them on inspection, for example, on the grounds that they are not in accordance with the agreed specification.

Many exporters have a marine insurance policy that covers all their export shipments and which can be extended to cover all modes of transport, reasonable periods of storage and specific risk factors such as damage due to extremes of cold or heat. Often the exporter will take out a floating or open policy which covers all his shipments so that all that is necessary is to advise the details of each shipment to your insurance company or broker. It is important to understand clearly your insurance policy and to discuss the details of the cover with your broker to ensure that you are properly covered. All shipment advice and any other information given under the requirements of your policy should be strictly and honestly provided. Inaccuracies in the information given can lead to difficulties with any claims. If you have a claim that exceeds the maximum (£1,000) that an insurer will settle without investigation, then a loss adjuster, who is independent, will be appointed. He will make a recommendation for the settlement of the claim.

Cargo insurance is usually underwritten using the marine all risks (MAR) policy form containing three sections of clauses. The section A clauses provide comprehensive cover for goods with certain inclusions whilst the sections B and C clauses only give limited cover. Discuss with your broker which clauses you require.

Importing risks

The main risks for an importer are connected with foreign exchange and the recovery of his money, e.g. if he has paid in advance and he finds the goods are not acceptable because of damage or for other legitimate reasons. The importer paying in his own currency has few problems with the currency exchange risk other than possible price fluctuations. However, should he be buying in a foreign currency then he can protect his own currency price by buying the foreign currency forward to be available when payment falls due or buying and putting on deposit. He can also take out options to buy the foreign currency which will also 'insure' him against a major adverse change in exchange rates. It is essential to discuss the foreign exchange risks with your bank if you are buying in a foreign currency.

Importers must ensure that the goods they buy are insured for CIF value plus 10 per cent – hence if they do not receive the goods or the goods are damaged they can make an insurance claim to recover their money. As soon as the importer is aware that the goods are damaged or have not arrived he must call in a loss adjuster to survey the damage. The importer is responsible for insuring the goods from the moment the title is transferred to him whether or not he has actual physical possession of the goods.

Product liability

Product liability is a worrying problem for many companies, especially SMEs. Product claims from consumers in the USA hit the headlines from time to time. Within the EC it is becoming a growing problem. Since the costs of defending an action or paying out substantial claims would be likely to bankrupt smaller manufacturers, product liability insurance must be considered. Your insurance broker should be able to advise you on the type of policy that will give you appropriate cover. An importer should also think about appropriate insurance.

Packaging and labelling

Although packaging might seem a very mundane subject, nevertheless it is a vital part of exporting. Export packages need to be designed to perform a function, to look attractive and to be cost effective. To perform effectively the package must be able to protect the product from damage, mishandling and the weather, i.e. rain, sun and if necessary extremes of heat and cold. The package should be capable of being lifted, stacked or moved with other smaller packages. The Institute of Packaging can give you advice on packaging and provide you with information on package designers and export packaging companies.

The movement of goods always subjects them to certain hazards such as vibration, sharp movement and heavy handling. It is not unknown for drums and other packages to be dropped over the sides of ships or lorries for further transit! In many countries in Africa, Asia and South America the roads are very rough and packages are likely to get a considerable pounding during long journeys.

It is important to limit the cost of packing both in terms of the materials and the time it takes to pack. However, packages must conform with any size and weight limitations imposed by carriers. In addition these factors can affect the freight charge. Packaging must also be such as to limit pilfering and yet look reasonably attractive when it reaches the customer.

A package can also have a resale or reuse value, particularly in developing countries. This should be taken into consideration when designing a package since it will be a selling point.

Labelling of packages for transit needs to be in accordance with internationally accepted codes and regulations, as well as any specific regulations applied by the importing country. There are also special requirements for dangerous goods. The labelling should be clear but not so attractive as to tempt pilferers and other thieves. It is also important to ensure that the products inside the packages are properly labelled. For example, there are food and pharmaceutical regulations in many countries with which you must comply or your products will not be cleared. The DTI country desks can advise on most regulations and where to get detailed help and advice, e.g. from The British Standards Institute.

Customs practice

Customs all over the world control the flow of goods in and out of their country, they collect duties and they record the movement of goods for statistical records for various government departments. Clearing goods through customs in most countries is a complex matter and you should employ a clearing agent. In the UK the Institute of Freight Forwarders can provide you with names of their company members who act as clearing agents. The Institute will also find clearing agents in overseas markets if you are selling on a delivered to customer's premises basis and have to meet all the overseas market's customs requirements.

HM Customs and Excise in the UK have available for exporters and importers a large number of public notices, i.e. booklets, which can be obtained free of charge from your nearest Customs and Excise office. Look at the list of notices and identify which ones you are likely to need. These notices will also tell you how to recover value-added tax (VAT), any other recoverable duties on exports and what you will have to pay on imported goods.

Exporters provide details of their exports to the Customs and Excise office by making an export declaration which describes their shipment and presenting it before their goods are shipped. This is known as a 'pre-entry' declaration. The alternative is for the exporter or his agent to register with the Customs and Excise to obtain a Customs Registered Number (CRN). This enables goods to be exported under the simplified procedure, i.e. a full export declaration can be lodged after the goods have been shipped but pre-shipment advice in the form of a commercial description must have been provided in lieu of the pre-entry declaration.

An importer bringing goods into the UK has to present to the Customs and Excise, at the place of discharge, a customs entry form. This is copy number 6 of the Single Administrative Document (SAD) set. You will also have a Customs Procedure Code (CPC) number which shows whether the goods are for UK use, re-export or further processing etc. You will also have to attach to your entry form certain other documents such as a form for goods liable for *ad valorem* duty, i.e. duty based on the value of the goods, plus some documents that should have been provided by your supplier, e.g. three or more copies of the original invoice. Make sure you have all the necessary information and documents to clear your goods from customs. This will also ensure that you do not overpay duties. If you have overpaid you can obtain a refund by means of an overentry certificate. If you have underpaid you will have to complete a port entry certificate (available from HM Customs and Excise), pay the additional duty and possibly a penalty!

Documentation

Detailed information on all the documents discussed below can be obtained from SITPRO and the Institute of Freight Forwarders. Small firms in general should use the services of freight forwarders to handle their shipments and to assist with the documents.

Single Administrative Document

In January 1988 a set of eight forms known as the SAD set was introduced to replace the many different documents in use between EC countries for international trade. The SAD set was specifically designed for use in the EC for export, transit and import purposes. Copies of the SAD set are printed by HM Customs and Excise and copies should be obtained from your nearest office.

TARIC

In January 1988, the EC also brought together the Common Customs Tariff (CCT) used for specifying rates of duty and NIMEXE – a separate and related system for collecting statistics. This integrated tariff system is known as TARIC.

Harmonized Commodity Description and Coding System

In addition a new common coding system to identify all goods and to satisfy the needs of international trade was introduced. This is known as the Harmonized Commodity Description and Coding System (HS). There are up to 15 digits in the commodity code. Each section of the code has a specific descriptive purpose and these are described in a booklet obtainable from the Customs and Excise office.

A full list of the commodity codes can be seen at the Customs and Excise office. It is complicated to understand and small firms should seek assistance from freight forwarders and other experts in order to ensure that they select the correct codes for their products from about 15,000 different headings. Customs and Excise offices, freight forwarders and major Chambers of Commerce should all have copies of the large three-volume customs tariff plus the updating customs notices. The commodity codes have to be used on all export and import documents and each different item has its own code.

Bill of lading

The bill of lading relates to the contract of carriage, i.e. the contract for the transport of the goods between the shipper and ship owner. It is evidence of a contract of carriage, a receipt of goods from the carrier and a document of title. The title to the goods can be transferred by the endorsement and delivery of the bill of lading. Bills of lading may be clean, claused, stale or through bills. A clean bill of lading has no notations on it and means the goods have been received and/or shipped in good condition and in the right quantity. A claused bill is used where, for example, the shipper has not verified that the goods are as described. In describing the goods on the bill of lading he will then use a clause such as 'said to contain'.

A through bill of lading covers shipments from the exporter's to the consignee's premises. It is used usually for a containerized shipment which may be going by various modes of transport.

Air way-bill

The air waybill is a carriage document issued by airlines to cargo shippers. It is not a document of title.

CMR note

The CMR note is an international consignment document which is required for the movement of goods by road. It is normally completed by the sender and travels with the goods to the destination point.

CIM note

The CIM note is an international consignment note for the movement of goods by rail. It is not a document of title and is non-negotiable. The consigner completes the note, blank copies of which can be obtained from the railway authorities.

Standard Shipping Note

The standard shipping note is a six-part document set covering the delivery of goods to a UK port. It is accepted by customs as a pre-entry document.

Parcel post

Small firms whose packages are below the size and weight limits for international parcels should use the Royal Mail International Parcels Service. SITPRO provide document sets known as post packs for sending goods by post. The *Post Office Guide* and the *Overseas Compendium* provide full information on the use of the parcel post for sending goods to individual markets. Details of recommended and forbidden packing materials for individual countries are given. However, you can now obtain standard collapsible parcel packages from your post office for use worldwide.

Other documents

Certificates of origin

There are two main types of certificates: the EC Certificate of Origin and the Arab–British Chamber of Commerce Certificate of Origin which is required for Arab League countries. These certificates have to be provided when they are called for on the sales contract, in LCs or in importation procedures in the receiving country. They are obtainable from Chambers of Commerce who will certify them when they are complete. In some cases they may also have to be legalized by the commercial section of the foreign embassy in London of the country to which your goods are being despatched.

ATA and Community carnets

The ATA and Community carnets permit temporary export and re-import of certain goods for special purposes and avoid the need for full import and export documentation. The Community Carnet is for countries in the single market and the ATA carnet covers 40 countries who are members of the ATA convention.

The goods generally covered by carnets are

1 goods for exhibition
2 commercial samples
3 professional equipment

The ATA carnets are available from the major Chambers of Commerce and the Community carnets are obtainable from Customs and Excise offices.

Not all documents have been listed above but these are the main ones that a small firm is likely to encounter. There are, for example, special documents concerning preferential duties for the export of EC goods into European Free Trade Association (EFTA) countries and certain African, Caribbean and Pacific countries. The customs notices will tell you which countries are included and what rules and documents apply. A freight forwarder can guide you through the complexities.

The Simpler Trade Procedures Board

SITPRO works nationally and internationally to simplify trade documents and procedures. It is an independent organization set up by the DTI.

SITPRO provides a broad range of services covering export documents and documentation systems. It has also developed computerized document systems and standards for electronic data interchange. SITPRO provides training for your staff in documentary procedures.

Anyone intending to develop their own in-house unit for handling documentary systems should contact SITPRO for information and advice. They have a register of approved SITPRO consultants who can assist you to establish approved systems (see appendix 5).

Importing

The importer generally receives the goods and the 'shipping' documents from the overseas supplier. However, he may arrange for the collection, carriage and delivery of the goods himself in which case he will be responsible for all the documents, clearing goods through customs and any export and import formalities.

If the goods are being sent to you and you are paying by LC, you have to state which documents you need and how they should be sent. Should you be paying by draft then the seller will arrange for the goods to be passed to you on payment of the draft at your bank.

As an importer you may have to prepare the customs entries, pay any duties or claim relief from duty. You may have your goods delivered to a duty-free area, i.e. a bonded warehouse or a warehouse in a freeport area, thus saving the payment of duties until you require the goods. Naturally there is a warehousing charge.

To clear goods through customs you will need to complete an entry form – normally SAD copy number six. In order to establish what duties you have to pay, you should consult the *Customs Tariff and Overseas Trade Classification* obtainable from HM Stationery Office. Your clearing agent will have a copy. There are fiscal, i.e. excise duties which are the same for UK-produced goods and customs duties. There are a variety of other duties some of which are payable on the custom's valuation. The latter is explained in detail in *Croner's Reference Book for Importers* but it should be noted that the valuation is based on the open market value.

Value-added Tax

VAT is chargeable on imported goods but not on services. It has to be paid at the time and place of entry. Your VAT office at HM Customs and Excise can supply you with public notices explaining all aspects of VAT on imports.

Quotas

Goods can be imported from many developing countries at preferential rates of duty. However, with certain sensitive goods for example there is a quota, i.e. a limited quantity that can be imported at this preferential rate. The *Customs Tariff and Overseas Trade Classification* part II gives full information on quotas, which also apply to imports of Japanese cars and some high-tech products.

Overall view

Delivering goods to customers in overseas markets not only means delivering goods safely and on time but also means ensuring that all the documentation is correct. The choice of the transport has to be made on the basis of minimizing costs and providing the buyer with the delivery performance he requires. Correct packaging and labelling are also a necessary part of making sure the goods arrive undamaged at the right destination. Importers must carry out their part of each transaction correctly.

Key points

- Delivery terms are vital – make sure you are familiar with the terminology.
- Make yourself familiar with the various transport modes, their advantages and disadvantages, so that you can make informed decisions about delivery costs and schedules.
- Package your products in a way that is appropriate for your markets.
- Familiarize yourself with customers and documentation procedures.
- Don't under-estimate the importance of insurance.

6

Setting up an export office

Outline

You may in time wish to set up a separate export or import office. This chapter analyses:

- the essential office equipment you will need
- the specific activity of an export unit
- the documentation it will need to process
- electronic communication
- training your staff

The export or import office is the hub of any company's international trade activities. Although in a small company the export unit may not be large, nevertheless there must be one person identifiably responsible for the export marketing and sales supported by someone responsible for the administration, i.e. systems procedures and documentation. A well-organized office is one of the keys to success in international trade.

In a small firm the export office will need to liaise very closely with those responsible for production in order to keep overseas agents informed of the despatch or delivery date against orders. They must work with the individual responsible for any technical information so that they can respond to technical inquiries. They must also pass on to research and development staff technical information about competitive products. Clearly the export office and the accountancy personnel also need to work closely together on the costing and pricing of orders. Particularly in a small firm the export unit must be an integrated part of the whole company.

Office equipment

These days no export office should be without its electronic equipment: a telephone with an answerphone, a fax machine, a telex for communications and a good photocopier. To type correspondence, to keep mailing lists and to maintain records of enquiries, orders and sales, a microcomputer–word processor with a good quality printer will be needed. A good filing system, a small library of reference books and a stationery store with all the blank documents are essential. Naturally the office should be furnished and decorated for comfortable and efficient working. Your agents and possibly some of your customers may well wish to visit you at your office so it should give an impression of quiet confident efficiency.

Office activities

The export unit has a significant planning role to play within the company. The following are some of the management activities for which it should be responsible.

It should prepare for the Sales Director

annual sales targets and forecasts
income and expenditure budget
capital expenditure budget
sales development plan
schedules for advertising and direct mail (with agents)
plans for sales and technical literature in foreign languages
overseas visit schedule including trade missions
exhibition participation plan (with agents)
training plan (for own staff, agent's staff and maybe customer's
   staff)

All the above plans need to be monitored and altered in response to actual results.

The export office should maintain the following:

enquiries and follow-up records
customer and product sales records
complaints record

agent and customer information files
competitor information files
orders in progress charts (with production personnel)
overdue payments charts (with accounts personnel)
product and market cost information
general market information files
despatch records
price lists by markets
quotation and invoice records by agents and/or customers

The office should also maintain a close liaison and good working relationship with

overseas agents
any direct customer
company's freight forwarder
company's shipper
HM Customs and Excise
packaging specialist
Chamber of Commerce
insurance brokers (with accounts personnel)
trade association export committee
bank (with accounts personnel)
customs and VAT offices (with accounts personnel)

The above lists are not exhaustive and a small firm should amend them to meet their particular requirements.

It is essential to keep realistic plans and effective records in order to be able to monitor and control the performance of the export sales activity. These records should be such as to be able to highlight any significant changes or trends in market conditions at the earliest possible moment. They should also indicate variations in seasonal activities in individual markets. Too much emphasis should not be placed on detailed changes since it is the overall aggregate results which matter most to the company. The main objective must be to ensure that the overall export sales are developing in accordance with the plans. Schedules should be kept up to date and next year's schedules prepared with plenty of time in hand for making detailed arrangements, including bookings, for exhibitions.

A record of all sales enquiries including Export Intelligence

dependent of one another so your forwarder needs to have a presence at each port you use in order to be able to submit information. Customs information on imports is also being handled electronically in ports like Amsterdam. Clearly the widespread use of EDI systems using EDIFACT standards would help the development of the free movement of goods within the single market as well as to more distant markets.

The benefits of EDI for transferring data from one computer to another without re-keying include

accuracy of data
speed of transfer
more efficient processing with fewer people
better customer service
more controllable business
closer cooperation between trading partners

More and more we shall see the replacement of paper communications by electronic communications for orders, invoices, booking requests, manifests, shipping instructions, delivery notes and statements. This kind of operation is currently most apparent to the general public when they visit a tourist agency or airline office to book and obtain a ticket for a flight.

Electronic documentation

Anyone proposing to computerize their import documentation needs a suitable software program that produces all the main export documents including invoices, packing lists, shipping instructions, standard shipping notes, certificates and the SAD. SITPRO have developed a suitable program known as SPEX 3. The SITPRO approved distributors for SPEX 3 are listed in appendix 5.

The SPEX 3 program has built-in links for transferring information to and from other systems, e.g. via EDI links using EDIFACT flexible formats. The second software package available from SITPRO is INTERBRIDGE the EDIFACT translator which is for the formatting and de-formatting of data and is designed to assist companies to implement EDI. INTERBRIDGE is capable of handling the largest and most complex of the EDIFACT messages. Both these software programs can be used on the majority of personal computers.

A number of software houses such as Beacon Management Services, who are an IBM independent software specialist, also offer software programs for export documentation. They are also adopting the EDIFACT standards.

Electronic mail

This is a system that enables you to transmit information, documents and messages from your computer screen to an electronic mail box, i.e. a computer store. An electronic mail box is specific to a recipient although you can have a mail box which any number of recipients can contact if they know the appropriate access code. There is also the teletex system which enables you to communicate with another person's computer via the telephone lines and which can replace telex between you and your agent. Anyone wishing to use these systems should discuss them with British Telecom and their computer supplier. As with all electronic communication systems using the telephone system, additional electronic hardware, such as modems, and software, i.e. operating programs, are required.

Training

All members of any export or import unit should receive training to keep them up to date and to improve their efficiency. Every year the training needs of each person should be identified, discussed with them, and plans made for them to attend appropriate short courses, seminars, conferences and exhibitions.

Chambers of Commerce

There are a significant number of organizations offering one- or two-day courses on the handling of documents such as LCs. The Chambers of Commerce are leaders in this field and whether you are an exporter or an importer you should contact them to ensure that you are kept informed of their course programme. They also organize seminars on trading with individual markets which will help to keep you and your staff up to date with changes. The larger the Chamber of Commerce, the greater the variety of courses they will offer including some especially for the smaller business.

Computer training

The computer software houses and the information database houses all offer free seminars to introduce you to their products as well as specific training courses for which there is a fee. Training in the use of word processors and microcomputers is now more commonly offered by the adult training establishments. However, most computer and word processor agents will offer courses on the use of their products – especially for new products. Office staff need to be trained to make the most effective use of all electronic equipment.

Professional institutes

Management and marketing seminars and courses in general or on specific topics are available from such organizations as the British Institute of Management and Chartered Institute of Marketing. The Institute of Export 1–3-day courses tend to be focused on export administration. All the professional institutes (see appendix 11) offer part time and distance learning courses leading to their qualifications. In general these are too time consuming for those managing small businesses. However, staff should be encouraged to take suitable courses to obtain professional qualifications relating to management, marketing and international trade. Other institutes offering specialist training in their sectors of international trade are the Institute of Freight Forwarders, the Chartered Institute of Transport, the Institute of Logistics and Distribution Management, the Institute of Chartered Shipbrokers, the Institute of Commerce and the Institute of Transport Administration.

Industrial lead bodies

There is now an Industrial lead body (ILB) for international trade to which the 'international trade' institutes belong. This ILB like those for other occupations is seeking to establish units and standards of competency and recognized national qualifications relating to training for various jobs. The Department of Employment's Training Agency have regional offices who can advise you of the existing available courses and progress in developing new courses, suitable for your staff. The Institute of Freight Forwarders can advise you of availability of approved Youth Training Scheme (YTS) training courses for any young people in your office.

The accrediting bodies for courses whose content is in accordance with an ILB's standards and units of competence is the National Council for Vocational Qualifications (NCVQ) who will agree a National Vocational Qualification (NVQ). Awarding bodies in the educational and training sector whose courses meet the requirements will be able to offer these national qualifications. These will be in addition to the qualifications awarded by a professional institute or educational establishment.

London Chamber of Commerce

The London Chamber of Commerce Examinations Board provides qualifications for courses in a number of areas of interest to the international trader.

They have a range of qualifications for secretarial courses including some which combine language competence with secretarial skills. The foreign language courses for industry and commerce (FLIC) are examined at four distinct levels and include a qualification for oral European and Asian languages used in the context of commercial transactions. In addition they are offering a qualification for courses which are aimed directly at people and companies who wish to extend their business activities into the single market. They also offer qualifications for a variety of courses dealing with other aspects of business all of which carry recognition from appropriate professional bodies and NVQs.

The courses are run at many educational establishments throughout the UK. A list of the places offering the courses, details of the syllabuses and regulations can be obtained from the Board's offices in Sidcup (address in appendix 13).

Language export centres

The LX centres have been established by the Department of Education and Science and the Department of Employment. Their purpose is to assist companies develop their export skills particularly for the European single market. They provide language training, export advice, consultancy services and cultural and orientation briefings relating to specific countries. Each LX centre is a consortium of colleges, polytechnics and universities often working in partnership with Chambers of Commerce and other organizations. A list of the LX centres is given in appendix 10. Small firms should contact their nearest LX centre to see what help and training might be available for their staff.

Department of Trade and Industry Enterprise Initiative

The DTI Enterprise Initiative is not a training programme. It provides up to 15 days' consultancy in marketing, design, quality, manufacturing systems, business planning and financial information. The consultancy meetings and report result in the company receiving information, advice and plans relative to their particular needs. The same results could probably be obtained through lengthy study and training, whereas the consultancy makes a more dramatic input towards raising a company's level of expertise and efficiency. Information regarding consultancy available under the DTI's Enterprise Initiative can be obtained from the DTI's offices.

Distance learning

Many small firms are not able to allow their staff time off for more than the minimal amount of training. However, this does not prevent the company from encouraging and helping staff to increase their knowledge and skills and to gain qualifications by following a distance learning course. Distance learning courses are also known as open learning courses, meaning that they are open to anyone to learn at his own pace at any time.

The Training Agency has produced a handbook *Ensuring Quality in Open Learning*. It explains the criteria for open learning and lays down guidelines to help providers and users of open learning material. A list of providers of open learning material can be found in the *Directory of Open Learning* also available from the Training Agency at Sheffield.

There are many courses available – for example, the Chartered Institute of Marketing now offers a series of open learning packages in marketing approved by the Training Agency. Henley Distance Learning Ltd offer two courses, one on export and marketing and the other on export procedures. The Open University and the Open College offer a very large number of courses including some relating to international trade.

There is no shortage of distance learning language courses available from such organizations as Linguaphone and Readers Digest. The DTI is also supporting the creation of a series of different language courses e.g. 'Make your Mark', a course in German for businessmen marketed by Pitmans.

Enterprise agencies

Local enterprise agencies are an excellent source of help and information on seminars and short courses for small firms. Some such as the London Enterprise Agency (LENTA) run export courses tailored to the special needs of small firms. The LENTA Export Enterprise course consists of two full day seminars including a syndicate session and five individual counselling sessions over the following six months. Small firm owners or a member of their staff are introduced to the basics of exporting in the following areas:

    market research
    market selling
    transport
    distribution
    documentation and administration
    terms of trade
    banking and finance
    methods and protection of payment
    sources of information

The enterprise agencies can also advise on importing, business plans, sources of risk finance and many other trading opportunities and aspects of running a small business.

Active Exporting Scheme

Active Exporting is a government-sponsored scheme to assist established SMEs to develop their export potential. The scheme is run by the Association of British Chambers of Commerce in conjunction with a number of leading Chambers of Commerce and two Export Enterprise Centres in Chelmsford, Essex, and Chatham, Kent. These organizations each employ a small number of Export Development Advisers. Initially the adviser will carry out an export audit which will include an assessment of your export training needs. This is followed by counselling sessions for which there is a nominal fee. This scheme like the DTI Enterprise Initiative Consultancies is highly subsidized.

Exhibitions and conferences

During the course of the calendar year there are world international trade and service exhibitions held at various exhibition centres in the UK, Europe and the USA. The major exhibitions often include conferences and seminars for visitors during the exhibition period. The World Trade Services Exhibition at the NEC in Birmingham each autumn is particularly useful for small firms who wish to bring themselves up to date on the latest services available to international trade. It also provides an opportunity to compare different companies offering similar services. International trade seminars also take place during this exhibition.

There are well-established international trade exhibitions held either in the UK or Europe which enable a small firm not only to see what their competitors are offering, but also to meet potential suppliers and sales agents in their industry. Usually seminars and conferences of technical and commercial interest to the attenders take place during the exhibition.

These exhibitions and conferences should be regarded as a training opportunity as well as a major source of information.

Key points

- Research the range of office equipment that is available.
- Make sure that the office is furnished with the necessary professional contracts, information, stationery and reference material.
- Consider how electronic documentation can help your business.
- Be sure to train your staff properly – remember your export office is the face of your business as far as your export customers are concerned.

7

Selling services

Outline

You may wish to sell a service rather than a product overseas.
This chapter covers:

- banking
- computing
- insurance
- professions
- exhibitions, fairs and conferences
- transportation
- consultancy
- agencies

The earnings from invisible exports make a major contribution towards the UK's balance of payments. Although there is a tendency to think of large companies like the major clearing banks in this field, there are in fact many small companies actively participating. Approximately 75 per cent of the employment in the UK is in the service industries of which many are directly or indirectly involved in international trade. The standard work which is a study of the export earnings of the service industries is *The Invisible Economy* (Pitman), a profile of the UK's invisible exports written by Professor David Liston and Professor Nigel Reeves. There is also a British Invisible Export Council which is responsible for promoting international trade in services. They publish a yearbook which contains much useful information.

The main gross invisible earners are

banking
insurance
tourism

shipping
civil aviation
royalties and other services
consultancy

The essential elements characterizing small firms in most of the above business areas are that they have a particular professional expertise or skill to offer and have identified a niche market whose needs they can meet.

Banking

The field of banking today contains very few small firms actually involved in banking. The few that do are most likely to be found in a special area of banking where expertise is at a very high premium. With the internationalization of banking any small firm providing specific expertise will automatically be drawn into international trade especially with the advent of the single market.

There are many small firms who provide special services to the banking world, notably those involved in supplying computer services, e.g. software, editorial work and advertising.

Computing

The computing services sector has been one of the fastest growing areas of international trade. Although the UK imports more than it exports this might change with the development of the single market and the growth in paperless trading. There are many small firms who supply computer services. They should seize the opportunities offered them internationally by worldwide growth prospects. English is the standard language for information technology and data processing so they have a built-in advantage over many other countries including those in the single market.

Small businesses in computer services should ensure when they are supplying multinationals in the UK that they also look into the possibility of supplying their overseas associates and subsidiaries. The experience they gain in the UK should enable them to determine the types of companies they are best able to serve. They should identify similar companies in overseas markets and approach them. The actual product sold, a tape or a disc, is small in price and value compared with the intellectual input into producing the software program on the disc. This can be shipped easily and cheaply by Royal Mail International Parcels and other express carriers such as TNT and DHL.

Small firms in this sector interested in developing their exports should contact such bodies as the local DTI regional offices and the Computer Services Association.

Insurance

The insurance industry is the largest source of the UK's invisible earnings. However, it is dominated by the large insurers and insurance brokers. It is very much an international business; however, there are still many small independent brokers providing services to companies and individuals. The small brokers are mostly involved in international trade when they are arranging cargo insurance or insurance for people travelling overseas. They may also become involved in providing insurance for foreign companies or individuals operating in the UK. It is likely that some small brokers will begin to form ties with similar brokers on the continent once all the national restrictions on cross-border insurance have been removed.

Professions

Accountancy, law, architecture and surveying are just some of the professions that have developed a significant activity in overseas markets. Small firms that have established footholds in the international business have in general achieved it by developing a specialist expertise. The accountancy firms have expanded into overseas markets through developing a greater range of financial services often associated with the requirements of an industry. Overseas auditing, tax planning, treasury management, company financial management and IT systems are all areas in which they have developed expertise. The legal profession has developed its international business in relation to areas such as banking, securities, acquisitions and mergers, shipping, aviation and real estate. They are also involved in general corporate and commercial work as well as litigation and arbitration. Some specialize in patent and trademark registration and licensing in the UK and overseas.

Architects have always been able to find work overseas if their work is of sufficiently high calibre and well known. Chartered surveyors' overseas earnings come from the use of their professional skills and advice in property valuations, acquisitions, disposals, and on-site management of developments.

In general business is obtained overseas by professional partnerships through their reputation and quality of service, personal contacts, discreet promotion and introductions. A knowledge of the laws and practices affecting their activities and the way they are allowed to operate is necessary in each market. Smaller professional partnerships have found it advantageous to form links with similar partnerships in certain overseas markets.

Tourism

Tourism represents a major foreign currency earner for the UK and provides employment for a large number of people. There are many small businesses in the tourist industry. It has been estimated that there are over 200,000 self-employed and working-owners in this sector alone. It is a very diffused industry; nevertheless it can be viewed as a number of sectors, namely

hotel and catering
leisure facilities and entertainment
travel and transportation
tourism organization
exhibitions, trade fairs and conferences

Small firms in the hotel and catering trade have been quick to absorb ideas from abroad, particularly menus of the day and more imaginative dishes. Larger companies have extended their activities overseas but few small firms have thought to link up with similar small businesses in Western Europe and North America. Considerable efforts have been made to raise standards in this sector of the tourist industry by better education and training. Training establishments in this field have also been able to contribute to our invisible earnings by attracting overseas students.

Small firms wishing to benefit from providing services to visitors from overseas should contact the British Tourist Authority (BTA) and their local English, Scottish or Welsh Tourist Board. Advice can also be obtained from the Hotel and Catering Industry Training Board and many of the leading educational and training establishments training people for this industry.

The leisure facility and entertainment sectors also offer many opportunities for small businesses to contribute to overseas earnings. Not only can the quality of what they offer attract overseas visitors but in the entertainment world there are always possibilities for taking the entertainment overseas. In addition extra overseas income can be earned through sales of videos and tape recordings in overseas markets.

Travel and transportation in the tourist field is very much concerned with moving people around with their baggage. Small coach operators should have no difficulty in finding groups such as members of an institute or a society who wish to pay a short visit to the continent. Similarly there are groups who wish to come to the UK and travel as a coach party. Developing business internationally is not difficult and should become much easier after 1992, when one hopes that customs barriers will disappear and there will not be the same documentation needs in the EC. Currently it is essential that anyone carrying passengers fully understands what he needs to be able to cross frontiers and travel in Europe.

Finding customers to take abroad or who wish to come to the UK can usually be done by promoting your company's services to likely users. Examples include tour organizers, local societies and other groups such as sports clubs in the UK and on the continent. It is essential to have a brochure illustrating your services and giving examples of contracts that you have fulfilled.

There are growing opportunities for small businesses who provide lecturers and tour guides. Quite often it is a small tourist agency that finds a special niche. However, the standards have to be high for both foreign tourists coming to the UK and for tourists from the UK going abroad. A good knowledge of some foreign languages is a definite advantage for those wishing to develop this type of international business.

The expansion in overseas travel has in turn led to a rapid growth in overseas holiday and tour organizers in Europe, North America and Japan. To enter this field a small company must already have or recruit people trained and experienced in operating a tourist agency. In view of the comprehensive on-line information service for bookings available from airlines and others all staff in a tourist agency must be capable of operating a keyboard with screen and printer. They must be capable of operating a service for both UK and foreign tourists and businessmen. Payments for services in foreign currencies will not be at all unusual. The management and staff must be aware of how to handle foreign exchange transactions and the foreign exchange risk. They will need to work closely with the foreign exchange section of their local bank.

The tourist agency will need to know the visa requirements and conditions of entry as well as the preferred, not just essential, health precautions to take for each country. They should also know the true merits or otherwise of the accommodation they arrange for their clients and the problems that may arise in certain countries and how they can be overcome. This applies not only to holding hotel reservations but also to entering and leaving some countries.

Exhibitions, fairs and conferences

Exhibitions, trade fairs and conferences provide many international business opportunities for small firms engaged in this industry. Exhibition organizers tend to be medium sized before they arrange exhibitions overseas. However, small exhibition organizers arranging them in the UK should be aware of how to market the exhibition to businessmen overseas and foreign visitors in the UK. The DTI's Fairs and Promotions Branch and the Chambers of Commerce can be good sources of advice.

Small businesses engaged in the design of exhibition stands should always look for opportunities to design stands for UK companies showing in exhibitions or trade fairs overseas, or foreign companies showing in the UK. They may need to link up with a local stand fitting firm, unless they contract to organize the stand fitting themselves.

Some small firms will contract to collect, take and bring back all the stand units, equipment, samples and literature required for an exhibition in the UK or overseas. Such firms will need to be fully aware of the documentation required, such as carnets, which allow the temporary importation of goods into a country without the payment of duties. Carnets are obtainable from the Chambers of Commerce. The Institute of Freight Forwarders and the Chartered Institute of Transport can advise on the vehicle documentation and any other documentation that may be required.

Transportation

There are a large number of small businesses involved in the transportation industry in areas such as freight forwarding, road haulage, clearing, broking and servicing. Many of them are involved in international transactions and have developed an expertise which is needed by industrial and commercial firms in their catchment areas. Their knowledge and skills are based on training and experience often gained with the help of their professional institute and trade association. Some of them such as the freight forwarders will have already formed links with clearers and forwarders in overseas markets. The single market, the growth in paperless trading, electronic communications and the Channel Tunnel provide challenges and opportunities for all the small firms in this industry. The main sources of information for these firms are their own trade associations, the DTI and other government departments, Chambers of Commerce and their own contacts within their industry.

Consultancy and other services

When consultancy is mentioned in relation to overseas countries the tendency is to think in terms of engineering design, construction and management contracts. In fact another major area is that involving education contracts and consultancies. Engineering design, construction and management contracts tend to become available as part of major projects often financed by aid funds. Details of these projects can be obtained at the indicative and tender stages from Export Opportunities Ltd (the EIS service) and the World Aid

Section of the DTI. Small consultancy firms can either seek to obtain business as a subcontractor or if it is available separately bid for only the consultancy part of the project.

Educational contracts and consultancies are usually handled by the Educational Contracts Department of the British Council. Many of the contracts in developing countries are funded by the World Bank and other development funds. Small consultancies, by joining with universities, polytechnics and other colleges, can often assist the British Council to put together a joint tender for a contract.

Health care also represents a major area for consultancies. Information on consultancy contracts in developing countries, frequently financed by aid funds but also sponsored by commercial companies, charities and other foundations, is not easy to obtain. The British Council, the British Medical Association, the British Health Education Council (BHEC) all have some information, but most small consultancy groups will find that they will have to develop their own sources of information for consultancies involving their specialized skills.

Frequently overlooked are the opportunities for designers to sell their services to companies abroad particularly in the USA and Europe. Small firms in the design and craft field, e.g. the design of jewellery and other high value articles, have built up and can build up successful businesses with major wholesalers and retailers in the industrialized countries. Interior designers by identifying big hotel, office and shopping projects through the Export Intelligence Service can secure contacts with whom they can seek business.

Consultancy is one way for small firms to develop their overseas business alongside their manufacturing or other services assuming there is a logical relationship.

Agencies

There are many small firms acting as agencies: as export and import agencies; as recruitment agencies; and as estate agencies. Already it is apparent that many of these agencies are seeing opportunities for business outside the UK but especially in the single market. Like any other organization an agency needs to carry out market research before attempting to establish a position in the market. You have a number of choices with regard to the way you might operate. You can appoint a representative, obtain an office and recruit suitable staff or form an appropriate association with a similar agent. It is possible to offer your services through appropriate advertising media such as specialist journals. However, it is essential that you make yourself aware of the local laws governing the operation and activities of an agency.

Key points

- To sell a service overseas you really need a particular type of professional expertise.
- There are many opportunities to sell services overseas but make sure you research these carefully and contact local agencies as well as professional advisers before committing yourself.

8

The single market

Outline

This chapter considers the emergence of a single market in Europe specifically. There will be great opportunities for small businesses in the run up to 1992 and some pitfalls. This chapter contains:

- an examination of the legislation which will affect business activities in Europe
- an explanation of the types of community funding that are available
- detailed analysis of all 12 member states

The completion of the single market by the end of 1992 with the removal of the great majority of barriers to trade within the EC will affect all small businesses. There are about 2.5 million small firms in the UK and all of them are likely to be affected to a greater or lesser extent in the years up to the end of the century. The same situation will have to be faced by small firms in the other 11 countries in the Community as more suppliers and new products, services and competition have their effect.

It is essential that all companies look at what the single market will mean to them. For example:

- Will they have an advantage or be at a disadvantage?
- To expand into Europe what actions should be taken?
- How will the existing market change?
- What will be the effect of any new competition?
- How can they benefit from the availability of any new products and services?
- Will customers' requirements change?
- Should they form links with other companies in Europe?

Undoubtedly there are other questions that the company should consider but the importance of the exercise lies in trying to analyse the effects of the single market on the company with a view to planning and taking action to meet the new challenges.

A company should look in detail at its overall strategy and its specific policies for its products, production, distribution, marketing, sales, personnel and finance. The need to keep up to date with pending and actual changes in laws and regulations affecting your business is paramount. Sources and lines of information need to be established so that you are alert to any problems or opportunities. The DTI has published a number of booklets on the single market and every small business should obtain them. They are available from the DTI Regional Offices and the Single Market Unit at 1 Victoria Street.

The Single European Act (SEA) commits the European Community (EC) to establishing a single market by 31 December 1992. The single market will then be an area in which there will be the free movement of goods, persons, services and capital in accordance with the provisions of the Treaty of Rome. In fact there are three European Communities all set up by separate Treaties:

European Coal and Steel Community (ECSC)
European Economic Community (EEC)
European Atomic Energy Community (Euratom)

The three together are commonly known as the European Community (EC).

Under the treaties, the Council and the Commission may make regulations, issue directives, take decisions and make recommendations or deliver opinions. Regulations apply to all member states and take precedence over national laws. Directives do not have legal force in member states, but require them to achieve a certain result in a specified period. If this is not achieved then particular provisions will nevertheless become effective. Decisions apply only to specific parties, i.e. member states, companies and individuals. Financial decisions are enforceable in national courts. Recommendations and opinions are only the views of the body issuing them and have no legal force.

A precise programme of action to complete the single market was prepared in 1985 and is being applied. Over 600 individual measures have been approved, are under discussion or are likely to be proposed. Companies and other bodies need to be very much aware of the measures that are likely to affect them.

Spearhead

Spearhead is the DTI's on-line database of information on the single market measures. It provides a summary of the state of progress with individual measures, but it also gives access to the full texts of relevant EC legislation. The latter information is held in the EC's own CELEX database. Companies can access Spearhead through Profile Information, a database system which is part of the Financial Times group of databases. The Export Network Ltd on-line information database also has a quick reference section that enables companies to identify easily legislation that will concern them. It also provides an in-depth analysis of legislation by each industrial sector and other major areas such as taxation, intellectual property and company law. The analysis clarifies the existing legislation and anticipates measures still to be introduced. The addresses of these database companies are given in appendix 12.

These databases can be accessed either directly with one's own equipment or via organizations such as Chambers of Commerce, public libraries and trade associations. The DTI also issue single market factsheets which deal with some of the more important areas of harmonization.

Harmonization

There are a number of legislative measures adopted, in discussion or proposed which are of general interest to companies. Different quality standards and safety requirements are a major hindrance to free trade and the EC have taken action to harmonize them. Over a hundred technical committees exist to establish common standards and methods of testing to meet the requirements of EC directives which establish essential requirements for health, safety, consumer protection and the environment. The British Standards Institute acts for UK companies who in turn have and need representation on all the committees. This representation is usually provided through trade associations.

Public purchasing accounts for some 15 per cent of the Community's gross domestic product. Although directives are in force in this area there are still many obstacles to fair trading.

The Commission have made changes to the Supplies Directive (applying to public supply contracts) by widening the rules to reduce the barriers. Similar steps are being taken with the Works Directive (covering public works contracts), and sectors currently excluded such as water, energy, transport and telecommunications are likely to be included. All these changes will open up the Community market to UK companies but will create more competition in the UK.

Freedom to work anywhere in the Community is one of the basic rights. Unfortunately, member states in the past have generally not recognized each other's qualifications. The Community has issued a general directive which in due course will make it easier for those in professions to practise anywhere in the Community. They have also issued some sectoral directives covering specific areas such as nursing. The Community through the European Centre for the Development of Vocational Training (CEDEFOP) is also establishing equivalence or comparability with the UK's National Vocational Qualifications. Their work has already covered several industrial sectors. Hence it is important that staff be given the opportunity to acquire qualifications that, if not already, may in time be recognized throughout the Community.

Intellectual property rights can be protected within the Community by applying for patents and trademarks in each individual country. There is also the European Patent Convention under which patents can be protected in most Community countries, the exceptions being Denmark, Ireland and Portugal. Some of the EFTA countries, i.e. Austria, Sweden and Switzerland, are also included in the convention. However, the Community is likely to adopt its own Community-wide conventions for patents, trademarks and copyright. A Community Trademarks Office is likely to be established but national trademark systems are likely to continue to exist for some years.

There is an existence some copyright protection throughout the Community as all member states belong to the Berne Copyright

Convention, and there is already a special Council directive protecting the design of semiconductor integrated circuits.

The Community has a common commercial policy covering trade relations with outside countries. There are common external tariffs which apply to imports into the Community of non-EC goods. The Community is not free to set all its own rules as it has obligations under the General Agreement on Tariffs and Trade (GATT) and the Organization for Economic Co-operation and Development (OECD). Companies can obtain information on developments in this area from the DTI's External European Policy Division. However, changes in external tariffs and regulations are also available from *Croner's Reference Book for Exporters* and *Tate's Export Guide*. Tate's information is available in book form or it can be accessed quickly via the Export Network Ltd database.

Progress has been slow in the consumer protection field and barriers and hindrances to free trade still exist between member states. However, a number of directives have been issued, namely those dealing with

misleading advertising
product liability
doorstep selling
consumer credit
toy safety
price indications

There are also a large number of environmental directives which are equally important. Companies should be aware of the directives which affect them and any further proposals that are being considered.

Structural funds

The Community has three funds administered by the European Commission which are intended to support the less developed regions in the Community. These funds are

European Regional Development Fund (ERDF)
European Social Fund
European Agricultural Guidance and Guarantee Fund (EAGGF)

Structural funds provide valuable opportunities for UK companies not only for developments in the UK but also as contractors bidding for consultancy contracts and for supplying equipment in other Community countries. Alongside the structural funds are the Integrated Mediterranean Programmes (IMPs) and a special programme for the modernization of the Portuguese Economy (PEDIP) financed by grants from the structural fund (a PEDIP budget line) and loans from the European Investment Bank (EIB).

Any company wishing to explore opportunities for funds or grants, or contracts financed by one of the above funds, should contact the DTI's World Aid Section.

The Export Network Ltd database provides information on contracts through its business opportunities section but it also has an EC-1992 section which gives information on grants, programmes and incentives. This section contains much useful EC information under the following headings:

1992 legislation (reference)	Summaries of EC directives by relevant industrial sectors
1992 legislation (analyses)	In-depth analyses of EC legislation by industrial and other sectors
Contacts	Lists of contacts in UK and Europe who can assist exporters with specific questions and consultancy requirements
Grants/programmes/ incentives	Latest EC assistance schemes
News	Changes in EC legislation and other matters affecting EC trade
EC central purchasing	Breakdown of the EC central budget and buying opportunities created by public spending

Small firms

The Community has a number of programmes to assist small businesses throughout the market. The EICs, of which eventually there will be 300 throughout the Community, provide information on public procurement contracts and advice on tendering procedures. They are also required to provide SMEs with information affecting

EC market intelligence, research and development programmes, finance and training. The Small Business Task Force in Brussels provides EICs with basic and up to date community documentation and access to certain EC databases. The centres help SMEs with Community contacts and applications to participate in Community programmes including helping with the formalities.

The Business Cooperation Centre (BCC) in Brussels was created by the Community in 1973. It was established specifically to encourage cooperation between companies within the Community. It provides advice and contacts to companies seeking partners. In 1988 it created the Business Cooperation Network (BC-Net) which is particularly aimed at SMEs. Essentially it is a computerized system which links a network of 400 business advisers throughout the single market. A list of the advisers in the UK who are known as 'intermediaries' is obtainable from the Small Firms and Tourism Division of the Department of Employment.

The intermediaries are the first point of contact for any SME interested in finding a partner for any type of business activity. This includes cooperative agreements, joint ventures, licences, franchises, subcontracting, agents, import and export arrangements, and mergers. The intermediary will offer (for a fee) some business planning advice and endeavour to find a partner through the network. A company or cooperation profile for an offer or a request is drawn up by the intermediary and this is fed into the BC-Net computer in Brussels. If a match can be found then both the requesting and offering companies are informed immediately. Should no match be found then all the intermediaries in a specified area are notified of the offer or request.

The advantage of BC-Net is that it brings companies together to participate in

Community research and development programmes
regional development and redevelopment activities
industrial cooperation outside the Community
transnational subcontracting
joint ventures

Financing for some of these activities may be available from the European Venture Capital Association (EVCA). The European Financial Engineering Company which was created by the Commission and the EIB also offer financial support for SME transnational ventures.

The single market countries

The single market consists of 12 countries and has a total population of about 325 million. Each country has its own characteristics and culture as well as individual regional variations. It is necessary to know and understand each country individually if an effective and long lasting business is to be built. Whilst a good agent will be your eyes and ears it is still necessary to visit each country regularly. The small business wishing to develop in the EC markets should obtain the *Hints to Exporters* for each country from its DTI regional office or the country desk as well as specific information relating to its industrial or service sector.

The following pages give a brief snapshot of some aspects of each country. Much more information will be required if you are planning to trade with any of the markets.

The Federal Republic of Germany and West Berlin

The FRG is one of the world's leading economies and the UK is its biggest trading partner. It has a population of over 60 million which enjoys a high standard of living. It is sometimes regarded as a difficult market in which to sell because of the need to provide quality goods with a high standard of service. A firm must develop its business in a meticulous manner if it wishes to succeed.

Although many German businessmen speak English a working knowledge of German is desirable. Correspondence and literature should be in German. There are significant regional differences between one part of Germany and another. Usually it is necessary to employ more than one agent to cover each region effectively. Many of the big stores and cooperatives prefer to deal directly with manufacturers others buy through commission agents. There are strict conditions regulating the terms of agreements with agents and these are likely to form the basis of EC legislation. The DTI German desk can supply information on agency agreements.

Almost all German imports have been liberalized; however, there are strict product and safety standards. Unlike the UK there are many bodies responsible for standards and for issuing safety certificates. The British Standards Institute THE are able to advise companies on the requirements for their products.

Payment by German companies is usually by open account or by bill of exchange with some credit. It is essential to check on the credit worthiness of any potential clients or customers. The UK debt collector organizations generally have agents in Germany and they can be used to collect debts.

Buying in the retail sector tends to be concentrated into the hands of major purchasing organizations and salesmen must be empowered to negotiate with buyers. The buyers expect a complete delivery-service to any point in Germany. There are organizations in the UK and Germany who will provide such a complete service.

Advertising to support your product is necessary and retail organizations may insist upon it. In general, because of the concentration of buying power German retailers have a greater hold over their suppliers than is the case in the UK.

Trade fairs are a very important element in the market. Some of them rank amongst the most important international exhibitions and fairs and buyers attend them from all over the world. Small businesses will find exhibiting with their agent or under the umbrella of a UK trade association as the best and least expensive way to participate as an exhibitor.

The Netherlands

The Netherlands is one of the most densely populated countries in the world with a population of about 15 million. Many of its inhabitants speak a language other than their own – usually German and/or English. Most business people speak English and it is therefore a fairly easy country with which to trade. It is the world's second largest agricultural exporter; this is based on its very intensive agricultural and horticultural industry. The country is heavily dependent on its international trade having hardly any natural resources. Nevertheless it has significant heavy engineering, chemicals, natural gas, textiles and light engineering industries.

In general Dutch businessmen prefer to deal with importers or exporters direct; nevertheless it is advisable to appoint an agent or representative. Any agency agreement is assumed to imply that it is an exclusive agreement for the area and products specified, unless it states specifically that it is non-exclusive. Detailed information on agency legislation is available from the DTI's Overseas Trade Division.

All prices should be quoted in the local currency, (guilders), CIF a Dutch port. Payment is usually by open account and can be very rapid if the Girobank system is used as this is very widespread in the Netherlands. Debt collection agencies are good and the major English agencies are represented. No business should be done without first checking on the credit worthiness of the potential customer.

There are no exchange control regulations and import and export regulations are minimal, mainly affecting agricultural products. The SAD documentation is in regular use and standard shipping documents for the transport of goods between the UK and the Netherlands. As might be expected the country has extensive bonded warehouses where goods can be held provisionally or temporarily stored. This makes the Netherlands a very convenient base for doing business in neighbouring countries, namely West Germany and Belgium. Dutch agents are familiar with trading in these countries and can assist UK companies to get established.

France

France is a founder member of the EC. Her industrial output is second only to West Germany and she has a population of about 55 million of whom more than a third are below the age of 25. Having very few natural resources the French have concentrated on developing their nuclear power industry as a cheap source of energy. Paris is very much the political, financial, commercial and distribution centre of France. Export and import business is very largely carried out by companies based in Paris.

There are no import duties on trade between the UK and France but value-added tax (taxe sur la valeur ajoutée (TVA)) is charged on most goods entering France. Import licences are not required for most UK goods but if they are required they must be obtained by firms or individuals established in the country.

Businessmen in France expect to conduct their business in French, more so for discussions than for correspondence. UK exporters should note that if possible all documentation should be in French as this facilitates customs clearance of their goods. If a company appoints only one agent he should be located in Paris; however, in some industrial and commercial sectors it is also necessary to appoint agents in other major cities to have adequate coverage of potential clients and customers. UK companies wishing to sell direct to major buyers, e.g. representing chain stores, must ensure that the buyer clears the goods and pays VAT or he must employ, as a legal requirement, a French customs clearing agent.

Prices should be quoted CIF a French port in French francs although for some products it may be necessary to quote delivered prices in order to be competitive. Most payments are made by bills of exchange but usually some credit has to be given. UK debt collecting agencies with agents in France will undertake the collection of debts but prior discussion with the agencies is essential. The same agencies or your banks can provide credit worthiness information on potential clients and customers. In view of the closeness of Paris to the UK and the development of the Channel Tunnel all small businesses interested in exporting should seek to develop business in France.

Spain

The population of Spain is about 40 million. It is a country whose economy has been growing rapidly and it is expected to gain considerably from its membership of the EC. It joined the EC in 1985 and whilst most barriers and quotas will be removed by 1992 it will have some special protection in certain areas for a few more years. To carry on business effectively in Spain it is necessary to have a working knowledge of Spanish. Trade literature must be in Spanish and correspondence should be in Spanish.

Spain has a strong agricultural and horticultural sector as well as a very diverse manufacturing industry. It is one of the major tourist countries in the world and has a large expatriate population in some coastal areas such as the Costa del Sol.

The imports of certain goods such as cotton garments and colour televisions are subject to quota restrictions and customs duties and taxes still have to be paid on many goods. The latest information can be obtained from the Overseas Trade Division of the DTI. Import licensing and foreign exchange regulations can be complex. Import documents are required under existing Spanish exchange control regulations for all goods valued at 500,000 pesetas or more. The applicant for these documents must be a legal entity in Spain, i.e. a Spanish company or an individual permanently resident in Spain. Without the appropriate import document money cannot be remitted abroad to pay for the goods.

All prices to Spanish buyers should be quoted CIF a Spanish port in the local currency, pesetas, or in some cases such as delivery by post as a delivered price, duty to be paid by the buyer. Bills of exchange are widely used for payment. At present agency legislation applies only to individuals as does the EC legislation; however, new legislation is expected for companies acting as agents. It is essential to have a good local agent who not only knows how to do business in your products but who also has good contacts in the government departments and can process documents properly.

UK importers should be aware of the safety standards and type approval requirements in relation to their own product specifications.

Denmark

Although Denmark is still regarded by some people as mainly an importer of agricultural products in fact their industry contributes more than three times as much to their gross national product. It is a country with a population of about 5 million, many of whom speak both English and German. Companies are willing to undertake negotiations and correspondence in English. Culturally it is different, e.g. it is usual to give and receive entertainment, to give gifts to one's hostess and on every occasion to express thanks for food and hospitality.

Denmark has few natural resources except for some oil and enough natural gas to last them until well into the next century. Manufacturing companies tend to be small and highly specialized. There are generally no restrictions on imports although value-added tax (MOMS) is applied to nearly all goods. There are also a number of special taxes on luxury goods. For certain products there are strict safety regulations and test certificates must be submitted to the appropriate board for approval.

Normally one agent is sufficient for the whole of Denmark and he is most likely to be situated in Copenhagen, the capital and commercial centre. Agency legislation is in line with the EC directive, but there is no standard form of agency agreement. Resident agents handle most imports but some of the large buyers representing large departmental and chain stores or some of the major cooperative groups prefer to buy direct from manufacturers.

Prices are usually quoted CIF a Danish port and delivered in Danish kroner. Credit of 30–60 days is normally expected and payment is by open account or by bill of exchange. It is essential to check on the credit worthiness of potential customers. The UK debt collection agencies have representative organizations in the country.

Transport between the UK and Denmark is excellent and RO/RO ferries operate regularly between the two.

Belgium and Luxembourg

Belgium and Luxembourg may be considered together as they have had an economic union for very many years. Luxembourg is French speaking whereas Belgium is French, Dutch and German speaking. Which language you need depends on which region is relevant to your business. French is spoken by most businessmen and English is often their second or third language. The population of Belgium and Luxembourg together is about 10 million. They are both densely populated and highly industrialized although Luxembourg is now a major financial centre.

Most UK goods can be imported without licences or duties. However, VAT applies to most products. It is not easy to find good agents in Belgium as most of them already have satisfactory arrangements with existing suppliers. Generally one agent is sufficient to cover this compact market in spite of the language differences that exist. The EC agency legislation covers agency agreements; however, it should be noted that the unilateral termination of an agreement can lead to possible penalties.

Prices are normally quoted in Belgian francs CIF Antwerp, Brussels or Luxembourg. Payment terms usually involve the granting of 60 or 90 days' credit. If cash payment by open account or bill of lading is required then normally a discount of 2 or 3 per cent will have to be conceded. In certain sectors extra special attention has to be given to the needs of buyers and your agent's advice and guidance is essential.

Transport between the UK and Belgium is excellent with regular

RO/RO ferries and container services between the two countries. Antwerp is one of the largest ports in the world. Travel by air, train or road presents no problems and small firms should choose whichever transport mode is the most convenient for themselves or their goods.

Importers will find Belgium an easy country within which to do business. Service companies will find that Luxembourg and Brussels present good opportunities for business, but exporters of goods will find that Belgium is a very competitive market.

Italy

Italy is a country of contrasts with the relatively rich industrial north and the impoverished south. There are substantial regional differences in social outlook and commercial practices which UK traders need to understand. Rome is the political and administrative centre whereas Milan is the commercial and industrial centre. Rome has a population of 3 million and Milan about 4 million. The total population is about 60 million.

It is advantageous to be able to correspond and speak in Italian and it is essential when doing business with SMEs. Most leading businessmen also speak English and/or French. UK traders should have at least one agent in Italy who usually would be based in Milan. If there is sufficient market potential then an agent should be appointed for the southern half of the country below Rome and possibly one also for Sicily. Italy has legislation governing agency agreements. A contract for an indefinite period allows an agent to claim an indemnity when it is terminated if he has not defaulted.

Prices usually have to be quoted in lire CIF or FOB. Many importers expect long credit terms of 120–180 days. The best system of payment is by documentary collection via your own clearing bank using a bill of exchange. LCs are not popular but it may be possible to get a bill of exchange avalised (guaranteed) by the bank in Italy. Exchange controls regulations are complex and frequently a problem and so you should discuss payment arrangements with your bank.

Deliveries to Italy from the UK are frequently made by road, rail and air as the ports are often congested and slow. Port charges can be high. Genoa is the largest port and Leghorn the largest container-handling port. Goods should be containerized where possible to reduce the risk of pilfering.

Selling in Italy is not easy because you are often dealing with a large number of small firms although some may be in cooperatives. Understanding the buyer's needs is essential and a good agent will advise you correctly how to respond to them.

Ireland

Agriculture is still the major industry in the Irish economy although the industrial base has been growing steadily. The population is about 3.5 million. Dublin, the capital city, is the main port and the industrial, trade and commercial centre.

There are no language problems for UK exporters but they should be aware of the cultural differences. An Irishman's outlook and opinions are often very different from those held in the UK. They are generally friendly, and time must be set aside to get to know one's agent and customers.

Agency agreements are governed by normal contract law and there is no difficulty in appointing an agent. One agent is normally sufficient for the whole country. Close cooperation with an agent is essential to ensure success.

Business is usually done on open account with the customer paying in Irish pounds or sterling on a CIF Irish port or delivered basis. UK debt collection agencies who also offer credit status reports operate throughout the Republic. UK banks can also readily provide status reports on Irish companies.

Travel and transport to Ireland represent no problems. There are frequent RO/RO ferries as well as container shipments and airline services. In general Ireland should be an easy market for UK exporters assuming that there is sufficient potential business. SMEs should not be put off by the apparent small size of the market compared with other Community countries.

Portugal

Traditionally the UK has been one of Portugal's major trading partners. It has a resident population of about 10 million but this is substantially increased in the summer months by a large influx of tourists. Lisbon the capital is the main centre for business but Oporto is the major industrial city in the north and is famous for its port wine trade.

The Portuguese have very formal manners and appreciate correspondence in Portuguese. However, most businessmen also speak English and French. Personal contact is of very high importance in business relationships and UK companies must meet their agents and customers regularly. In general suitable agents can be found in Lisbon and Oporto. There is no special legislation affecting agency agreements although at least six months' notice is normally expected for the termination of any agreement. Companies should not attempt to have a single agent for Spain and Portugal combined.

Portugal is a major recipient in Europe of overseas aid from the World Bank, the EIB and EC regional development funds. The DTI World Aid section can provide information on these funds and on how to pursue business under aid-funded contracts. The EIS via Export Opportunities Ltd (who also collect aid information from other sources) provide indicative and tender information on aid projects. Your Portuguese agent will need to have a good local contact with aid fund representatives and the relevant government departments if you wish to be considered as a supplier. Also you will need to be registered as a supplier with the aid fund principals and have contact with them to ensure you receive the relevant tenders.

Transport between Portugal and the UK has been considerably improved by the introduction of a weekly RO/RO ferry service between the two countries. Direct road transport facilities are available and express parcel carriers are also extending their services to the country.

Prices usually have to be quoted CIF a Portuguese port in escudos or sterling but 90 days' credit is frequently expected. The British–Portuguese Chamber of Commerce in Lisbon and other agencies offer a debt collecting service.

Greece

Greece is one of the newest members of the EC as well as one of the poorest. It has a population of 10 million that speak modern Greek. Most businessmen also speak German, French or English. A knowledge of some modern Greek is invaluable for anyone wishing to do business in Greece. Like Spain and Portugal Greece has an extended period beyond 1992 in which to harmonize some of its rules and regulations with those of the rest of the EC.

The agricultural industry is still the main industry in Greece, although the manufacturing industry, which is dominated by SMEs, is growing slowly. Invisible export earnings from tourism, shipping and remittances from migrant workers are very important to the economy. The capital Athens is the main commercial centre.

There are no problems in appointing agents in Greece although good agents are not easy to find. One agent may be sufficient for most of Greece; however, if your products are likely to be of interest throughout the country, then additional agents should probably be appointed for northern Greece, and Crete combined with the Dodecanese Islands. As Greece receives considerable aid under the EC regional funds, principals and agents should look for opportunities under aid-funded project contracts.

Prices should be quoted CIF a Greek port in sterling or US dollars although some business, e.g. public sector tenders, must be done in the local currency, drachmas. It is most important to ensure that customers and clients are able to pay for your goods and services. Cash against documents and LCs are common terms of payment. LCs often involve a credit period of up to 90 days and in exceptional cases up to 180 days. Debt collection agencies are not active in Greece and it is not worth seeking to recover anything but large sums through the legal system.

Key points

- Find out what effect the competition of the single market is likely to have on your business.
- Gather as much information as you can about EC legislation, the harmonization proposals and qualification requirements.
- Make sure that you protect your company's rights.
- Funds *are* available – you should explore the possibility of getting grants for your international activities.

9

The rest of the world

Outline

There are, of course, many attractive business opportunities outside Europe. This chapter explains:

- the role of the various international bodies that govern trade relations at an international level
- the role of world finance groups
- the need for cultural sensitivity in international business
- the European Free Trade Association
- opportunities in the world's major markets including, North America, Japan and the Pacific Rim, Africa and the Middle East and the Eastern bloc

Although the single market should be the prime target for many small businesses, the rest of the world still offers some very good opportunities. Small firms in the high quality craft and design field may be surprised to find that top departmental stores and specialist shops in the USA and Japan are interested in their products. Others selling specialized products which can be used in most countries might well find that they can develop business in many different parts of the world. Established consultants will find there are plenty of opportunities for business in developing countries.

Many UK importers already have a well-established trade with many countries outside Europe, and new small businesses should not have too much difficulty in finding reputable suppliers of goods and services in the developed countries of the rest of the world. Business with developing countries can be more hazardous. Selection and grading of products, abiding by specifications, packing satisfactorily and adherence to delivery dates are all problems that are more likely to occur with developing countries than others. This is mainly because of the lack of employee training in many of these countries. In general payment for goods should be arranged so that it is not made until they have been received and inspected.

Protectionist policies practised by various countries, often in the mistaken belief that they are the right way to assist their own business to develop, too frequently restrict international trade. Too often, as in the USA, protectionist policies result from political pressure from self-interested groups who can see no other ways of gaining time for the development and modernization of their manufacturing industries and services. The sudden imposition of such policies can have a fatal effect on a small business engaged in international trade unless they can quickly change to trading in other products, or in other countries. The EC operates protectionist policies in relation to such products as textiles where the multi-fibre agreement restricts textile imports. The restrictions on imports of agricultural products and the common agricultural policy also distort production and prices to the disadvantage of the consumer and create difficulties for the international trader.

International bodies

The rules that govern trade relations between countries are agreed at international rounds of negotiations. These are set out in GATT and are hopefully improved in each round of negotiations. The latest negotiations are known as the Uruguay Round. Except for most centrally planned economies and a few developing countries all countries are members of GATT. In the past negotiating rounds, attention has been focused on promoting free trade in all manufactured goods, but in the Uruguay Round attention is also being given to free trade in services. Agreement has been reached on the main principles of the Services Agreement. The terms on which service suppliers will be given access to markets are being worked out by the Group of Negotiations on Services (GNS). However, these will have to respect individual national laws and regulations applying to services. Those exporters and importers of services in the UK should be watching for the results of the GATT negotiations, the directives affecting services in the EC and the changes in UK laws and regulations.

There are two other organizations which play an important role in relation to GATT. The OECD has a membership of 24 industrial countries. It provides an information and advisory service to members on the development of trade and has established a code of conduct for multinational companies. The UN Conference on Trade and Development (UNCTAD) is a forum in which developing countries are in the majority and which discusses trade and aid matters of particular interest to the developing countries. A joint venture between GATT and UNCTAD is the International Trade Centre (ITC) which endeavours to help developing countries improve their trading activities and promote their exports. It has been responsible for the Generalized System of Preferences (GSP) under which industrialized countries grant tariff concessions on some manufactured goods from developing countries. The integrated programme for commodities was also established to create international commodity agreements (ICAs) to stabilize commodity prices by financing buffer stocks etc.

World finance groups

There are many international agencies' funds for economic development in developing countries – a list is given in appendix 6. The World Bank group of funds play a predominant role. The group consists of the International Bank for Reconstruction and Development (IBRD), its affiliates the International Development Association (IDA) and the International Finance Corporation (IFC).

The IBRD is responsible to those nations who provide the financial resources. Each subscribing country's voting power in turn depends on the size of its subscription to the Bank. Most of the resources come from borrowing from richer countries paid for at commercial rates. Hence developing countries are in turn faced with high interest rates on their borrowings from the bank. However, the bank provides 'soft' loans via the IDA which are for 50 years, interest free, and require no repayments for the first ten years. These loans are for the very poorest countries. Most of these bank loans are for large-scale government projects for energy, transport and water.

The IFC's role is to encourage private enterprise projects in developing countries. It purchases shares in new ventures as well as those that require further development, e.g. textile mills in Africa. It raises capital on the international market and sells its investments to other investors.

The World Bank group are a natural target for both manufacturers and consulting firms as indeed are the other fund agencies listed in appendix 6. Neither manufacturing nor consulting firms should attempt to obtain business unless they are established. Very small firms particularly in the consultancy field are unlikely to be considered. However, specialist small manufacturers should definitely look for opportunities, e.g. those in specialist engineering sectors. To find out how to bid for business financed by international agency funds, small businesses should contact the World Aid Section at the DTI and attend one of their regular free briefings. Consultancies will need to register with the agencies although fortunately registration with the World Bank Data on Consultants (DACON) system covers many of the funds. Forms for World Bank registration can be obtained from their offices in London. Manufacturers need only register as suppliers with a few of the funds such as the African Development Bank Group. Registration does not guarantee business, nor does no registration exclude a company from bidding for business.

To bid for business it is important to recognize that borrowers in the developing countries select and contract the business, or have a strong influence on the selection. Projects under the European Development Fund, for example, will be put out for tender by the department known as Director General VIII of the Commission in Brussels but borrowers in the developing country will have agreed beforehand on specifications etc. to be included in the tender, thus possibly limiting potential bidders.

The European Development Fund is sourced by the EC countries and is used to aid those African, Caribbean and Pacific countries who are members of the Lome Convention. As with other funds it is important to have good relationships with the technical advisers and officers responsible for tendering at the fund's headquarters. It is equally important for your agents to have good contacts with the fund's representative and government officials in the countries which are benefiting from fund-aided projects. All aid fund organizations issue indicative programmes for projects which are to be funded. Your agent and you should be aware of these programmes and follow them through where a project is of interest, by submitting an offer or by seeking subcontract business with whoever gains the contract.

Bilateral funds operate very similarly to international funds but for this business your agent should keep in close contact with the British Embassy or similar foreign aid representatives in the recipient country. This will enable your agent to determine whether he can obtain orders for your goods or services financed by an aid fund.

Export Network Ltd via their on-line database system, or Export Opportunities Ltd (EOL) via first class post, electronic mail, telex or fax, can keep you advised of international fund agencies' call for tender, including invitations to prequalify. Subsequently they will provide the names and addresses of firms, notified to EOL, who have been awarded contracts or have submitted bids for tenders. Taking the information from EOL is an easy way to start seeking business that is fund aided.

Other challenges

The great variety of markets in the rest of the world calls for an understanding of the differences in language, culture, politics and religion. In some countries such as Australia, New Zealand, South Africa and the USA it is relatively easy to do business. Although there are always some risks in these countries, they are not fraught with the risks that exist in some of the developing countries. The political and commercial risks are very high in some of the latter countries and it is essential to have credit insurance that covers both these risks. It is also essential to ensure in advance of despatch that payments will be made, by confirmed irrevocable LC or by one of the aid fund agencies – usually by LC. Unfortunately fraud is very common in many parts of the world so it is essential to check that all the documents you receive are genuine. Even if you are doing business with developed countries such as the USA be aware of the different attitudes to payment that exist especially if you are not being paid by LC. Regrettably some buyers will use any loophole you leave them to avoid or delay paying.

When dealing with the rest of the world a businessman will very quickly discover that countries that intensely dislike each other may attempt to stop you trading or travelling to the countries they dislike. Israel and South Africa are the two countries where the most problems currently exist. If you trade with either of these countries do not reveal it to their unfriendly neighbours. Should you visit them make sure you have separate passports for these two countries. Avoid having airline tickets, passports or other documents which show that you are visiting or have visited these countries. Should you also be visiting an unfriendly country they may confiscate your tickets and return you home. These are not the only two countries where there are difficulties in trading and travelling and an international traveller should always be on the alert for this type of problem.

The Middle East Association can advise you of the problems that occur in trading with Israel and other countries in the Middle East. In particular they will be able to give you up to date advice on the activities of the Central Boycott office in Damascus which seeks to identify companies helping Israel and to stop Arab countries trading with these companies. This is known as the Arab Boycott. If you make products or provide consultancy in the defence sector you will find that not only the UK but also the USA have restrictions affecting with whom you may trade. The DTI and the Defence Sales Organization (part of the Ministry of Defence) can advise and assist you to sell your products overseas.

The following sections give examples of the opportunities and challenges that are met in selected markets in the different regions of the rest of the world. There are some very major differences between markets and between regions and in the content of this book it is not possible to go into great detail. Anyone wishing to look at the potential for their products in a particular market or region should contact the country desks in the DTI and other sources of information.

The European Free Trade Association

The EFTA countries – Sweden, Norway, Finland, Iceland, Austria and Switzerland – are natural markets with which to develop business especially if you are already successfully established in some of the European Community countries. Most businessmen in these countries speak English as well as their own languages and German. All the countries have become concerned at the effect the single market is likely to have on their economies. As a result each of the EFTA countries has special agreements with the EC whereby trade in industrial products between EFTA and EC countries is, with few exceptions, duty free.

All the countries are demanding markets; however, a good agent will give you guidance. He should be supported by a sales representative who visits him regularly and becomes fully conversant with the needs of the market. Some companies operate without agents and just employ a sales representative but this really depends on your type of business.

Iceland is the smallest of the six countries and lacks the modern industries possessed by the others. There are no difficulties in transacting business in any other countries but the usual precautions should be taken to be reasonably sure that you will be paid for your goods and services. Norway is one of the richest countries in the group with very considerable revenues from the oil and gas fields in the North Sea. Switzerland is also a very wealthy country.

All these markets deserve careful study before entry in order to ensure that there is sufficient potential business to make an export effort worthwhile. In general one will be expected to trade either by open account or by bills of exchange and to quote delivered terms rather than FOB or CIF although CIF terms will be more acceptable than FOB terms. German competition is very strong in most of these territories and it is essential to maintain high quality, good design, first class delivery performance and competitive prices.

North America

The USA and Canada are the most attractive areas for UK exporters and importers after the single market. However, anyone contemplating exporting to the USA should be aware of the risks involved if their products cause injury or damage. The question of product liability should be discussed with an insurer before exporting. It is also important to know whether or not your goods will be subject to Federal or State regulations governing quality, safety, and any other technical or special requirements. Appropriate seals of approval may have to be obtained from a standards body before the goods can be sold. Most goods also have to be marked with the English name of country of origin. There are also regulations governing the labelling of certain products.

There are many different ways of marketing in North America. Importers and distributors will often buy on their own account and market the product themselves. Commission agents or representatives will act as salesmen to collect orders which are then placed directly with their principal, i.e. the manufacturer. Sales can also be made direct to many customers either by visiting them regularly from the UK or by selling to their buying house in London. Many multiple stores and departmental stores maintain buying houses in London and a list can be obtained from the DTI country desk. Mail order is big business with both retail customers and manufacturers. Some of the mail order and catalogue houses have representatives in the UK with whom you can discuss business. The mail order business in the USA is dominated by five big companies, four of which are based in Chicago. It is not only retail products but also industrial products such as electronic equipment and parts for other products which are sold by mail order.

In choosing agents in the North American markets it is important to bear in mind the vast distances between major centres as very few agents will be able to cover all areas. At least two and possibly three agents will be required to cover the USA and similarly in Canada. In the USA separate agents will probably be required for the East Coast, the Middle West and the West Coast.

North American importers generally buy on credit terms. Unfortunately the risk of non-payment is higher than one might expect. Credit status reports and trade references should always be taken up. Protesting of unpaid bills and use of debt collectors is essential if losses are to be avoided. Bankruptcy and similar situations are regarded more lightly than in the UK.

Australasia

Australia and New Zealand are natural countries for UK companies to look at if they wish to trade further afield than the single market. They both have a sophisticated economy and enjoy a high standard of living. Agriculture is of major importance in each country and contributes significantly to their export earnings. Mineral resources are of major importance in Australia while New Zealand is particularly strong in energy resources. The manufacturing industries in both countries are limited by the small size of their home markets. The UK has substantial investments in both countries and Papua New Guinea. UK clearing and merchant banks have substantial operations in Australia and Lloyds Bank has a major subsidiary in New Zealand.

Australia and New Zealand have many regulations controlling the quality, safety and purity of many products. In Australia there are frequently differences between the Federal and State requirements and between States. It is rarely necessary to appoint more than one agent in New Zealand but this is not always the case in Australia. A few agencies will have full coverage throughout Australia but more often than not it will be necessary to appoint several agents each with their own specified territory.

Importers expect to pay in sterling CIF or FOB, by a bill of exchange or even by open account. It is therefore essential to check on the credit status of potential agents and customers and to use debt collecting agencies or for large amounts, the legal system to collect unpaid bills. Because of the distances involved even more care is required in ensuring that your customer is reliable and will pay you than might be required in the UK.

The Far East

Japan, South Korea and Taiwan are the most important trading countries in the Far East. All of them have a very substantial favourable balance of payments and are slowly opening up their markets to imported goods and services. Language is a barrier to trading but finding a good agent who speaks and writes English is not too difficult. Cultural differences are significant; for example, always take plenty of brochures and a large supply of business cards when visiting these markets. Business cards will be studied closely and it is important to reciprocate by studying their cards. If possible your name should be printed on your visiting card in local characters.

The Japanese act very differently from many Western businessmen. They rarely make important decisions as individuals. They will ask many questions but will not make immediate decisions as they have a system of consensus decision making. Any proposal has to be considered by a number of managers and even if they agree your proposals they may still re-open negotiations with you. However, if they do re-open discussions they may simply be trying to get better terms even though they may already have agreed amongst themselves to accept your offer. The Japanese find it very impolite to say 'No', so be sure that when they say 'Yes' to your offer they really mean it. They may be saying 'Yes' because they understand what you are saying. Politeness and patience are essential in Japan. Quality requirements and packing specifications are exacting. Your products will be rejected if standards are not maintained.

There are a number of ways of selling in the Japanese market and the Japan External Trade Organization (JETRO) in London can provide you with information and some assistance. This is essential as the Japanese distribution system is very complex. In general you can sell directly to the large department stores, via the large general trading companies, via the specialist trading companies, or via a Japanese manufacturer who has complementary products. Buying from Japan is not difficult as they have large and very well-organized trading companies that between them sell most Japanese products.

In Korea and Taiwan it is essential to find reliable agents; if necessary use foreign firms with established offices in the countries. Price quotations often have to be in US dollars so action needs to be taken to protect your payments from the exchange rate risk. Payment is normally by irrevocable and confirmed LC.

The People's Republic of China is also potentially a major market for certain UK goods but there are political and commercial risks and credit insurance should be obtained to cover both risks. Nearly all imports and exports from China are handled by state trading corporations. Whilst there are severe limitations on private trading it is possible to use overseas trading companies situated in Hong Kong and Peking as your agents. Business with China is usually only obtained after long and persistent efforts. Payment is normally by irrevocable LC. It is not usually possible to have Chinese LCs confirmed, but the Bank of China has a good record for keeping to its obligations.

North Africa

The Moslem countries of North Africa from Morocco in the west to Egypt in the east have a long history of trading with Europe. Egypt is the most important of these countries and like Morocco and Tunisia is a fairly easy country in which to do business as long as your payment is secure. Algeria and Libya have centrally planned economies and much of the business is placed via tenders. Great care should be taken if visiting Libya because of the authorities' unfriendly attitude to people of certain nationalities.

Egypt is the largest of the North African countries, with a population of over 50 million. English and French are widely spoken. Industry is still dominated by public sector organizations with textile manufacturing being the most predominant. However, there is a growing private manufacturing sector in textiles, plastics and engineering products. Egypt is also a producer of oil and natural gas which contribute to its balance of payments. Tourism has always been important, the attraction being the ancient culture. Facilities for leisure tourism are now being developed.

Egypt like the other North African countries is a recipient of multilateral and bilateral aid and loans. All business in Egypt and the other territories should be conducted by irrevocable confirmed LC. It is necessary to have agents in Egypt which should be either one of the state trading companies or private companies or individuals. All agents must be registered with the Ministry of Economy and Foreign Trade. Prices usually have to be quoted FOB a UK port or CIF Alexandria. Payment terms generally have to include the granting of credit but this should be restricted to a maximum of 180 days or less for most products.

Algeria and Libya and to some extent Egypt ask for bid and performance bonds for tender business and care should be taken to ensure that no grounds are given for the calling of bonds.

Morocco is also a potentially attractive market for the UK. It has a very close relationship with France. There are advantages in using an agent with French connections especially as it may be necessary to accept payment in French francs.

The Middle East

The oil producing countries of the Middle East have been a target for the UK exporters ever since the oil crisis increased their revenues substantially. Turkey, Iran and Iraq have the largest populations. Turkey has had associations with the West for many years and, although it has no oil, it has valuable mineral and agricultural resources and has industrialized rapidly. It has also been the recipient of much aid and many loans particularly from the USA. Turkish businessmen usually speak English, German or French but the great majority of the population only speak Turkish. Foreign currency is in limited supply and is normally allocated on the basis of the FOB value of goods. Payment is usually by LC valid from the date of issue of an import licence. There are special arrangements for the allocation of foreign exchange if cash against documents (CAD) or cash against goods (CAG) terms have to be quoted. It is essential to understand the system for the issuing of import licences and the allocation of foreign exchange fully before doing business in Turkey. Your agent in Turkey and your UK bank should be able to guide you so that you can be reasonably confident of being paid, assuming that all your documentation is correct.

Iran and Iraq present considerable opportunities and yet considerable hazards for UK exporters. In general no business should be undertaken with either country unless your payment is by irrevocable LC. Both countries apply stringent foreign exchange and import controls and the bureaucratic systems must be fully understood if business is to be transacted successfully. The political and commercial risks are high and it is essential to have credit insurance for both risks. Agencies in both countries are strictly controlled by rules and regulations as most business is handled by the public sector. Neither country is easy to visit and visas are essential.

Saudi Arabia and the Gulf States offer good opportunities for business and in general there is no shortage of hard currency – much of the business is with public sector companies and tender and performance bonds are likely to be demanded. Israel, Syria and Jordan also offer good opportunities for business but all are short of hard currency and operate strict controls over the allocation of foreign exchange and imports. Agents can be appointed in all these countries without too much difficulty. French and English are commonly spoken by businessmen in Syria. English is more common in Israel and Jordan. It is most important to keep your business transactions with Israel completely confidential and quite separate from any with neighbouring Arab countries, because of the activities of the Arab Boycott committee.

The Pacific basin

Indonesia is potentially the most important country in the Pacific basin with a population of over 160 million. It has large reserves of oil and natural gas which are the backbone of its economy providing a substantial proportion of its domestic earnings and export revenues. Strict import and foreign exchange regulations apply and the method of payment is by irrevocable LC. The government of Indonesia will not allow confirmation of LCs. All imports are subject to inspection by SGS Inspection Services Ltd in their country of origin. In addition counter-trade requirements are in force with respect to many contracts particularly in the public sector. The UK has a counter-trade purchase agreement with the Indonesian government which lists products available for counter-purchase. Good local agents are hard to find. Some Indonesian companies have purchasing agents in Singapore and other centres.

Hong Kong, Singapore and Malaysia all provide excellent opportunities for UK traders because of their historical connections and close ties with the UK. English is the language most widely used in business in these countries and it is not too difficult to find satisfactory agents. Payment should preferably be by confirmed and irrevocable LC. Many international companies tend to use Hong Kong or Singapore as the regional centres for their business in the Pacific basin. This is partly because communications with the UK, USA and other developed countries are excellent and partly because of the availability of good office staff.

Two other countries in the region which should not be ignored are the Philippines and Thailand. The former has long been under the influence of the USA and continues to receive considerable financial assistance from that country as well as from other aid agencies. Many major USA companies are active in the Philippines.

It is essential to have an agent in the country. Thailand is a prosperous agricultural country but industrialization has been proceeding at a rapid rate and tourism is important. Most industry is privately owned and situated around the capital Bangkok where one should have an agent.

All imports into Thailand have to be paid for with foreign currency purchased on the open market. Exchange control is operated through the issues of certificates of payment without which foreign currency cannot be remitted. Payment is normally made by irrevocable LCs and prices are usually quoted CIF Bangkok.

Eastern Europe

The Eastern bloc countries are all centrally planned economies although very slowly private enterprise is beginning to play a more important role. The method of trading is via state trading companies. Because of the absence of freely exchangeable foreign currency most export trade with the UK is transacted in a hard currency or by counter-trade. Deals involving counter-trade have always been very important in trading with the Eastern bloc. Vienna and London are major centres for companies arranging such transactions.

Most of the Eastern bloc countries' trade with the developing world is transacted in bilateral clearing arrangements often involving their own aid funds. These bilateral arrangements provide opportunities for switch deals whereby goods are provided by a third country and naturalized before delivery. This occurs when the Eastern European partner is unable to supply some of the products required by the developing country.

Until recently it was not possible, except for a few special cases, to have an agent in an Eastern European country. The state trading companies have to be visited regularly and technicians sent out to explain the technical merits and the use of products to technical staff in factories and other organizations who are carrying out technical appraisals. Attendance at major fairs and exhibitions in Eastern European countries is essential as this is often where orders are placed. It is also an excellent method of gathering information about market requirements.

To begin exporting to Eastern European countries it is essential to consult the country desks in the DTI, to meet other organizations already exporting to Eastern Europe and to contact the relevant embassy in the UK. If there is a trade delegation visiting the UK it is worthwhile meeting them. It will be necessary to supply full details of your company to the state trading corporations and full technical information of the products you wish to sell. Responses will be slow but it is essential to follow up regularly and develop your contacts if you wish to secure orders.

Southern Africa

South Africa is the most prosperous country in Africa and dominates the economy of Southern Africa. It is rich in agricultural and mineral resources and has a well-educated and efficient managerial class, which comes from all sections of the population! Economic pressures have forced the pace of industrialization of the country as well as the education and training of its population. The slow integration of the black population into the political, social and economic life of the country is the cause of serious problems due to outside pressures and the activities of terrorist organizations.

There are no problems in finding good local agents in South Africa. English is normally used in business negotiations although Afrikaans is also an official language. It is important to check that a proposed agent has a complete coverage of the country. If not, then local agents should be appointed in one or more of the main provincial centres. Regular visits should be made to the market to support the agents.

Many South African companies have buying offices or buying representatives in the UK. It is quite common for South African companies to use confirming houses in the UK who will pay cash for goods for discounts or pay by a term bill. If selling direct to a buyer in South Africa then it is frequently necessary to grant up to 90 days' credit.

Other countries in Southern Africa such as Angola and Mozambique are still recovering from the ravages of civil war. Zimbabwe, however, is still reasonably stable but business should be done in all three countries by irrevocable confirmed LC.

Sub-Saharan Africa

The countries of sub-Saharan Africa are generally poor and under-developed. The largest is Nigeria which has about a third of the population of the region. Some of the countries are very rich in minerals and/or oil and have valuable agricultural resources. All of them are subject to political and commercial risks and business should be done by irrevocable and confirmed LC. Credit insurance for both commercial and political risks should also be obtained. All receive aid and loans from the international fund agencies.

Nigeria with its population of about 100 million and its rich agricultural and oil resources should be the most prosperous country in the region. Unfortunately owing to the shortage of trained and able management, a problem that also exists in all the other countries, it has not been able to develop its full potential. For similar reasons it is not easy to find good local agents in Nigeria and it is frequently necessary to employ the services of foreign trading companies with branches in the country. Much of the private trade in Nigeria is in the hands of large companies who have buying offices in the UK. Many of them were established with foreign capital and hence foreign ownership but nowadays they must have at least 40 per cent Nigerian ownership and Nigerian participation.

Corruption has long been a problem in many of these African countries (as well as in many other parts of the world) and great care is required when doing business. In order to overcome some of the problems many of the countries employ inspection agencies such as SGS Inspection Services Ltd and Cotecna International Ltd (see appendix 14). Nearly all imports into Nigeria and some other countries are subject to preshipment inspection for quality, quantity, price comparison and legality. Price comparison causes a lot of ill feeling because there are often very good reasons for differences in prices between customers and particularly between countries which the inspection agencies may not accept. The inspection agencies should be notified of the prices etc. as soon as you receive an order so that any problems can be cleared before you manufacture the goods.

Nigeria and Ghana and the East African countries such as Kenya, Uganda, Zambia and the Sudan have long had close ties with the

UK. They are all good countries in which to do business provided that you do it carefully and accept payment by confirmed and irrevocable LC. The only exception to confirmation is payment from some of the aid or loan funds but wherever possible you should seek confirmation of LCs, if necessary paying the fees yourself.

Some West African countries still have close ties with France and their currencies are often supported by the French franc. They are of increasing importance. Business is usually conducted in the French language and it is advisable to find agents with French connections as payments are normally made in French francs. The Ivory Coast is the most important of the countries, being the world's biggest producer of cocoa and a big producer of cotton and rubber. It also has offshore oil and gas fields which are almost sufficient to meet its own needs.

Importers will find that the biggest difficulties in trading with sub-Saharan countries are to ensure continuity and quality of supplies. However, in some sectors these problems have been overcome and careful researching with the help of UK government agencies and consultants to find reliable suppliers can prove fruitful.

The Indian subcontinent

The Indian subcontinent has long been attractive to international traders in the UK. Because of its period as part of the British Empire it has acquired many of the UK customs, and English is its business language. All the countries in the subcontinent are heavily populated and poverty is widespread. India has attempted central planning but with the cooperation of private enterprise. It has built up major industries behind protective barriers and these and its other policies of protectionism have caused and still cause difficulties for many exporters. The Indianization of foreign-owned trading companies has made it more difficult to find good agents. Many of the wholly owned Indian trading companies lack the financial and other resources to be able to cover the whole of India and great care should be taken in selecting agents.

Pakistan and Bangladesh, the other two important countries on the subcontinent, like India have essentially rural populations. Both have large natural gas reserves but Pakistan is more industrialized. Much of the industrialization in both countries has been carried out

133

by public sector companies but the first moves to privatization have now been taken in Pakistan. Both countries like India have five-year economic and social plans which give some indication of export opportunities.

Import and foreign exchange controls operate in all the countries in the subcontinent. All of them are complicated and should be understood before attempting to transact business. No shipment should be made unless the importer has a valid import licence.

Prices should usually be quoted in sterling and payment accepted only by irrevocable and confirmed LC unless other guaranteed systems of payment are offered. Commercial and political risks should be covered in your credit insurance policy. All the countries receive substantial aid in the form of grants and from time to time the UK will make available bilateral aid under the Aid and Trade Provision arrangement.

Many UK companies have a long history of importing from the subcontinent and either you should import via one of the existing import houses in the UK or you should at least take the advice of those with many years of experience. It is essential to find reliable suppliers in the subcontinent if you wish to do your own purchasing. There are both UK and EC regulations governing the imports on certain goods and these should be checked with the DTI as there are import quotas for products such as textiles.

Latin America

Latin America is a vast region with great natural resources and rapidly growing populations in countries such as Brazil and Argentina. The language is usually Spanish or Portuguese, two very similar languages. It is essential to be competent in one if you wish to develop your business satisfactorily – just as it is if you want to expand your business in the Iberian Peninsula in Europe. In fact there are close links between the two parts of the world and it is possible to find companies in Spain and Portugal who will help you do business in Latin America.

Brazil is generally regarded as the country with the greatest potential in Latin America although Argentina and Mexico are also important. These three countries like most countries in Latin America have serious balance of payments problems and large overseas debts and are dependent on grants and loans. Most of them suffer from high inflation. It is normal to quote for business in US dollars on an FOB basis although sterling quotes are accepted.

LCs are not normally used for payment in Brazil because deposit requirements make them very expensive. Importers usually pay on the basis of CAD. All imports are subject to the grant of an import licence by CACEX, the foreign trade department of the Bank of Brazil, who exercise tight control over all transactions. Those involving credit must be registered with the bank. Argentina exercises tight controls over its imports and all imports must be authorized by the Foreign Trade Department. Permission to buy foreign exchange must be obtained from the Central Bank. All exports from Argentina have to be paid for by LC and the foreign exchange sold by the exporter to the Central Bank.

Mexico operates two exchange rates, a controlled rate and a free market rate. The former is used for foreign trade transactions and the latter for individual exchange transactions, tourism and profit repatriation. Much business is done on a CAD basis and it is essential to check on the credit worthiness of buyers. Credit is frequently demanded and it is essential to have credit risk insurance. Non-accepted bills must be protested within two working days after presentation. Accepted bills must be protested within two working days of maturity date.

It is not easy to find good agents in any Latin American country. If possible use should be made of UK, Spanish or Portuguese company representatives such as those of ICI Tradeways. Should this not be feasible then try selling through some of the general merchants.

Key points

- Make contact early with the various international organizations and world finance groups.
- Don't overlook opportunities in the EFTA countries in the excitement of EC integration.
- Be prudent in your financial dealings with developing countries.

Appendix 1: Conditions of sale (export trade)

1 General

(i) The acceptance of this tender includes the acceptance of the following terms and conditions, and no alteration, variation, departure therefrom or addition thereto shall affect or be binding upon us, unless agreed in writing.

(ii) Acceptance of the tender must be accompanied by sufficient information including confirmation of issue of the Import Licence, where applicable, to enable us to proceed with the order forthwith. Otherwise we shall be at liberty to amend the tender prices to cover any increase or decrease in cost which has taken place after acceptance as a result of the failure to supply the required information. Any letter of credit established must be varied accordingly.

(iii) In cases where a tender has not been given it is nevertheless to be understood that the acceptance of any order by us is subject to the said terms and conditions.

(iv) In the event of a purchaser's order containing conditions it is understood that such conditions shall not govern this contract in any way and that the order is accepted subject only to the terms and conditions mentioned herein.

(v) We reserve the right to subcontract the whole or part of manufacture.

(vi) Unless previously withdrawn, the tender is open for acceptance within the period stated therein or, when no period is so stated, within 60 days after its date.

2 Cancellation

Orders received and accepted by us shall not be subject to cancellation either wholly or partially without our consent in writing. If such consent is given we reserve the right to make a cancellation charge where it is in our opinion fair, reasonable or necessary to do so.

3 Inspection

All products manufactured by us requiring a test are carefully inspected and tested by our own staff before despatch and except in the case of products already tested and finished the final test and examination at our works may, if so desired, be made in the presence of the purchaser's representative without extra charge therefor provided that such representative attends at our works for this purpose within a period of seven days after we have notified the purchaser that we are ready. In the event of approval of design or examination of the product during construction by an external authority being required, these will be charged for extra unless such examinations have been definitely specified and included in the price.

In any case it is to be clearly understood that these tests and examinations are not to delay the progress of work in manufacture.

4 Storage

If we do not receive forwarding instructions with the purchaser's order or within 14 days of notification to the purchaser that the products are ready for delivery,

(a) we shall remove the products to storage until such time as the purchaser can accept delivery and charge to the purchaser as an extra the net costs of transporting and storing the products

(b) the products shall be deemed to have been despatched 14 days after we shall have notified the purchaser that they are ready for delivery and then Clause 10 (Terms of Payment) shall operate in respect of such products.

5 Delivery

(a) Delivery will be made FOB at the port stated in our tender unless otherwise agreed.

Unless otherwise specified in our tender, packing in accordance with our standard export practice is included in the FOB price.

(b) Alternatively, delivery may be made CIF by arrangement with us and in this case the port will be stated in our tender. No lighterage, landing charges, dock, wharf or custom dues will be included. Freight and insurance charges will be based on the rates obtainable at the date of our tender. If these rates increase or decrease from any cause between the date of the tender and the date on which the goods are shipped, the contract price will be increased or decreased by the net amount of the increase or decrease due to the variation of such rates.

(c) Where a time for delivery and/or completion is specified, every endeavour will be made to adhere thereto but no liability whatsoever shall attach to us for delay in delivery or completion.

(d) Any time named for delivery unless otherwise specified by us shall date from receipt of final particulars including establishment of import licence, approval of drawings etc.

6 Commissioning and assembly on site

Our standard tender does not include for commissioning and assembly on site. Any such work is to be the subject of an additional contract, separate from the contract for the supply of the products.

7 Performance

In view of the numerous factors outside our control in respect of performance of the products, no liability is accepted for the performance, efficiency or fitness for any particular purpose of the products unless a definite guarantee in writing has been arranged on an agreed bonus and penalty basis, in which case the penalty shall be payable as liquidated damages. The purchaser is responsible for stipulating correctly the capacity and performance required from the equipment within the terms of Clause 1(ii).

8 Guarantee

(i) We undertake to replace by delivery FOB at the port stated in our tender any part which we agree to be defective and which has to be replaced arising solely from faulty material or workmanship and disclosed within a period of six calendar months from the date of purchase.

(ii) For the purpose of this condition the date of despatch is to be taken as the date when the product leaves our works or 14 days after we have notified you that the product is ready, whichever shall be the earlier.

Provided that:

(a) Notice in writing is given of any such defect immediately it is disclosed and no repair or replacement is made or attempted otherwise than by us, or with our express written permission;

(b) All materials and fittings supplied by subcontractors shall carry the subcontractor's guarantee, beyond which we accept no responsibility;

(c) Save and except the supply of the replacement part, we shall not be liable for and the purchaser hereby expressly agrees to indemnify us against any liability attaching to us at Common Law or under any Statute or Regulation or Order made by Competent Authority in respect of any claims, loss, damage or expenses directly or indirectly due to or caused by or consequential upon the existence or occurrence of any such defect or for any personal injury or damage to property attributable thereto;

(d) This guarantee and undertaking is in lieu of and excludes all other guarantees, conditions, warranties, representations and liabilities whatsoever, whether expressed, implied, statutory or otherwise, which might exist but for this provision;

(e) Any liability on our part is subject to the terms of payment and all purchaser's other obligations to us under the contract being strictly observed.

9 Price variation

The contract price is based on the cost of material, labour and transport ruling at the date of tender, and if between that date and the completion of work, variations, either by rise or fall, occur in those costs, then the contract price shall be amended to provide for these variations.

10 Terms of payment

Terms of payment are as stated in our tender. All payments are to be made in full, no discounts or deductions whatsoever being allowed unless otherwise agreed. We reserve the right to charge interest of 3 per cent above current base rate with a minimum of 8 per cent per annum upon all overdue accounts.

11 Illustrations etc.

(a) All descriptive and forwarding specifications, drawings and particulars of dimensions submitted with the tender are approximate only and the descriptions and illustrations contained in catalogues, price lists and other advertisement matter are intended merely to present a general idea of the equipment described therein and none of those shall form part of the contract.

(b) All drawings and designs and other information submitted in connection with the tender or any contracts arising out of it will remain the vendor's property and be subject to recall at any time; they are submitted in strict confidence and for the sole purposes of the tender, the contract and subsequent maintenance of the equipment; none of the drawings or designs or written matter, nor any of the information contained in them or otherwise supplied may be loaned, copied or otherwise communicated to any third party, nor may any use be made of them for any purpose whatsoever except for the purposes of the tender, the contract and subsequent day to day maintenance of the equipment.

12 Special risks

We are not responsible for any consequences whether direct or indirect of war, invasion, act of foreign enemy, hostilities (whether war be declared or not), civil war, rebellion, revolution, insurrection or military or usurped power, riot, strike, lock-out or civil commotion.

13 Patents

The purchaser warrants that any design or instruction furnished or given by him shall not be such as will cause infringement of any letters patent, registered design or trademark in the execution of the purchaser's order and shall indemnify the seller against all costs and damages arising from breach of this warranty.

14 Legal construction and interpretation

(i) The contract and these conditions shall in all respects be subject to English Law.

(ii) The titles of these conditions shall not affect their legal construction.

(iii) The expression 'purchaser' wherever used in these conditions includes any person for whom work is undertaken or to whom materials are supplied and the expression 'purchase price' wherever used in these conditions shall be construed accordingly.

Appendix 2: Agency agreement (example clauses)

THIS AGREEMENT is made the   day of   199

BETWEEN

(hereinafter called 'the Company') whose principal place of business
is at   of the one part and
(hereinafter called 'the Agent') whose principal place of business
is at   of the other part
WHEREBY IT IS AGREED as follows:

Appointment of agent

1 The Company hereby appoints the Agent as the exclusive agent of the
Company's for the purpose of securing orders in the countries referred to
in the First Schedule hereto (hereinafter called 'the Territory') for the
products factored and/or manufactured by the Company which are specified
in the Second Schedule hereto (hereinafter called the 'Products').
2 The appointment of the Agent hereunder will commence on the date
hereof and subject to the provisions for termination hereinafter contained
will continue for a period of . . . years and thereafter unless and until
terminated by either the Agent or the Company giving to the other not
less than . . . months' notice in writing expiring at the end of the said
period or at any time thereafter.

Obligations of the agent

3 The Agent hereby undertakes throughout the period of this Agreement:
ment:

3.1 to use his best endeavours to promote the sale of the Products to
customers of sound commercial standing within the Territory only
and to regularly inform the Company of his activities in this respect
and of the progress and development of the market for the Products

within the Territory and of all regulations affecting the import sale use and erection of the Products therein;

3.2 to maintain a permanent office and staff in the Territory and to pay all expenses whatsoever connected with the Agent's activities hereunder including stationery and all travelling expenses;

3.3 to deal only with customers within the Territory and not to solicit orders for the Products from customers outside the Territory provided that this shall not prevent the Agent (with the prior consent of the Company and subject to such terms as commission and otherwise as may be agreed with the Company) dealing or soliciting orders from customers outside the Territory in respect of Products for sale in the Territory;

3.4 not without the prior written consent of the Company to become directly or indirectly concerned engaged or interested in the sale distribution supply or manufacture of goods competitive with the Products;

3.5 not to disclose other than to the Agent's employees any trade secret or information of a confidential nature disclosed to the Agent by the Company hereunder and to ensure that this provision is observed by the employees of the Agent. This obligation shall survive the termination of this Agreement and upon such termination the Agent will return all specifications drawings and other data to the Company or its nominated representatives;

3.6 not without the prior written consent of the Company to enter into any contract nor make purchases nor incur any liability on behalf of or in any way pledge the credit of the Company or any subsidiary or associated company;

3.7 to transmit to the Company all enquiries for the Products as soon as they are received by the Agent;

3.8 not to assign transfer or charge in any manner whatsoever this Agreement or the Agent's rights hereunder without obtaining the previous consent in writing of the Company;

3.9 to communicate with the Company in English and to translate into English any information or material transmitted or communicated by him.

Terms and conditions of trading

4 The Agent will not make any representation or warranty with regard to the Products other than such representations or warranties as may from time to time be included in the advertising and promotional literature

143

specifications and other material to be supplied to the Agent pursuant to this Agreement.

5 The Agent will endeavour to obtain business (except where otherwise specifically authorized by the Company in writing or by cable) on the basis of the Company's normal Conditions of Sale as notified to the Agent from time to time, and subject to payment by confirmed irrevocable Letter of Credit or such other payment terms as may be agreed.

6 When requested to do so by the Company, the Agent will endeavour to obtain payment of accounts due to the Company and the Agent shall promptly remit in full to the Company without any deduction whatsoever all such sums as the Agent obtains.

7 The Company will have the absolute right in its entire discretion as it thinks fit to accept or refuse to accept any order of the products transmitted to it by the Agent. The contracts in respect of all orders obtained by the Agent and accepted by the Company for the sale of the Products will be made between the Company and each customer direct, unless the Company otherwise agrees.

Commission

8 The Agent will be paid by the Company a commission in respect of orders for products accepted by the Company and paid for:

8.1 where the order is from a customer in the Territory and is for supply and/or erection (or supervision of erection) in the Territory, the commission will be as specified in the first column of the Third Schedule hereto;

8.2 where the order is from a customer outside the Territory for supply and/or erection (or supervision of erection) within the Territory and the Agent can satisfy the Company that he has been materially instrumental in obtaining the order, the commission will be as specified in the second column of the Third Schedule hereto;

8.3 where the order is from a customer in the Territory for supply and/or erection (or supervision of erection) outside the Territory and the Agent can satisfy the Company that he has been materially instrumental in obtaining the order, the commission will be as specified in the third column of the Third Schedule hereto.

9 Should special circumstances require commission rates different from those specified in the Third Schedule, such rates will be subject to a special arrangement between the Company and the Agent preferably prior to the submission of the tender.

10 Subject to this Clause the relevant price for the purposes of calculating the commission will be the Company's ex works price (excluding amounts attributable to freight, insurance, packing, taxes, export and import duties and custom charges) for the products concerned which is effective when the order is accepted. If the said ex works price is increased or reduced by reason of any subsequent change in the specification then the commission shall be calculated on the increased or reduced ex works price as the case may be. The commission payable to the Agent may also be reduced where the said ex works price is reduced for a reason other than a change in specification, and in any such case the Company will advise the Agent preferably prior to the submission of the revised price to the customer but where time precludes this the Agent will be advised of the amount of commission included in the revised price.

11 The commission will be remitted in the manner and at the times specified in the Third Schedule. If any bills in respect of which commission has not been paid are not met at maturity the amount of commission payable to the Agent will be reduced proportionately; and any overpayment of commission will be immediately refunded by the Agent or may (at the Company's option) be deducted from any subsequent payment due from the Company to the Agent.

12 After termination of the Agreement, any commission due to the Agent in respect of orders accepted by the Company before termination will continue to be paid pursuant to the foregoing provisions as if the Agreement had remained in force. No commission will be paid to the Agent on any order accepted by the Company after the date of termination.

13 The Company will send to the Agent copies of all quotations orders acknowledgements and invoices sent by them to customers in the Territory for the Products. Where such documents specify a price other than that on which the commission of the Agent is based, the Company will inform the Agent in writing of the relevant ex works price for the purpose of calculating the commission.

Advertising

14 The Products will be promoted and advertised only under or in relation to the name of the Company and under such other names as may be specified from time to time by the Company. The Agent will not have any right to use the name of the Company in any manner as a description or name of his business. The Company will provide the Agent with such advertising and promotional literature and material as the Company

considers necessary. In directions and instructions (if any) as may be such advertising will be paid for by the Agent unless otherwise agreed in writing by the Company.

Patents

15 The Agent will not either during the continuance of this Agreement or thereafter claim any right or property in any patents trade marks trade names copyrights and designs in relation to the Products or in any literature supplied to the Agent hereunder; nor will the Agent register or cause to be registered in any part of the world any patent trade mark name copyright or design similar to or a colourable imitation of any patent trade mark trade name copyright or design which is the property of or subject to the control of the Company or any parent or associated company of the Company.

Assignment

The Company reserves the right, notwithstanding anything to the contrary herein contained:

16.1 in the event of its business or any part thereof (being a part concerned in the manufacture of the Products or any example thereof) being transferred to any other company to assign its rights and obligations under this Agreement to that other company after giving one month's notice of such assignment in writing to the Agent;

16.2 to vary the Second Schedule hereto defining the Products either by the withdrawal therefrom of the class or classes of goods named therein in the event of the Company ceasing to manufacture that class or those classes of goods or by the addition thereto after consultation with the Agent of a further class or classes of goods of the Company.

16.3 if in the opinion of the Company the Agent is not at any time producing adequate sales coverage throughout the whole of the Territory and without prejudice to any other of its rights under this agreement either to vary the extent of the Territory so as to exclude from this Agreement such part or parts of the territory as it thinks fit or to vary the Second Schedule hereto so as to exclude from the Agreement such one or more of the class or classes of goods therein set out as it thinks fit or to take both these courses of action save that neither such course of action shall be taken without the Company notifying the Agent promptly thereafter.

Termination

17 Without prejudice to any rights or remedies which the Company may have against the Agent the Company shall be at liberty by notice in writing to the Agent forthwith to terminate this Agreement if the Agent shall have a receiving order in bankruptcy made against him or shall enter into any composition or arrangement with his creditors or in the case of any event equivalent under the laws of the Territory or if the Agent shall cease or threaten to cease to carry on his business.

18 If the Agent shall be in breach of any of the provisions hereof on his part to be observed and performed and shall not remedy such breach if capable of being remedied within 21 days of being notified of such breach by the Company then the Company shall have the right by notice in writing to the Agent forthwith to terminate this Agreement on or after the expiration of such 21-day period. If such breach is not capable of being remedied the company shall have the right by notice as aforesaid forthwith to terminate this Agreement.

19 It is expressly agreed between the parties hereto that the Company shall not be liable to pay to the Agent any compensation arising as a result of the termination of this Agreement for any cause whatsoever.

Law

20 This Agreement shall in all respects be governed by and interpreted in accordance with the Laws of England and the Agent hereby submits to the jurisdiction of the English Courts.

Notices and communications

21 All notices and communications (by writing, telex or fax) will be addressed to the party concerned at the address of such party first above written or any other address communicated in writing to the other party as being effective for the purpose of this Clause.

AS WITNESS the hands of the duly authorized agents of the parties hereto the day and year first written above.

The first schedule

(The territory)

. . .

. . .

. . .

The second schedule

(The products)

. . .

. . .

. . .

The third schedule

(Commission)

(1)	(2)	(3)
Commission for orders accepted from customers in the Territory	Commission for orders accepted from customers outside the Territory for sale or erection in the Territory	Commission for orders accepted from customers inside the Territory for sale or erection outside the Territory
. . .	. . .	. . .
. . .	. . .	. . .
. . .	. . .	. . .

Payment of Commission   . . .

SIGNED for and on behalf of)
the Company in the presence)
of:)

SIGNED for and on behalf of)
the Agent in the presence   )
of:)

Appendix 3: Department of Trade and Industry regional offices

Northeast

Stonegate House
2 Groat Market
Newcastle upon Tyne   NE1 1YN
Tel: 091 232 4722
Tlx: 53178
Fax: 091 232 6742

Yorkshire and Humberside

Priestley House
Park Row
Leeds   LS1 5LF
Tel: 0532 443171
Tlx: 557925
Fax: 0532 421038

East Midlands

Severns House
20 Middle Pavement
Nottingham   NG1 7DW
Tel: 0602 506181
Tlx: 37143
Fax: 0602 587074

West Midlands

Ladywood House
Stephenson Street
Birmingham   B2 4DT
Tel: 021 631 6181
Tlx: 337919
Fax: 021 643 5500

South West

The Pithay
Bristol   BS1 2PB
Tel: 0272 272666
Tlx: 44214
Fax: 0272 299494

Southeast

Bridge Place
88–9 Eccleston Square
London   SW1V 1PT
Tel: 01 215 5000
Tlx: 297124
Fax: 01 828 1105

Reading (area office
for Berks, Bucks, Oxon, Hants
and Isle of Wight)

40 Caversham Road
Reading   RG1 7EB
Tel: 0734 395600
Tlx: 847799
Fax: 0734 502818

Portsmouth (satellite office)

SE Hants Chamber of Commerce
27 Guildhall Walk
Portsmouth   PO1 2RD
Tel: 0705 294111
Fax: 0705 296829

Cambridge (area office for Cambs, Beds, Herts, Essex, Norfolk and Suffolk)

Building A
Westbrook Research Centre
Milton Road
Cambridge CB1 1YG
Tel: 0223 461939
Tlx: 81582 DTIEAO
Fax: 0223 461941

Norwich (satellite office)

The Norwich and Norfolk Chamber of Commerce and Industry
112 Barrack Street
Norwich NR3 1UB
Tel: 0603 761294
Tlx: 975247
Fax: 0603 633032

Chelmsford (satellite office)
The Essex Business Centre
Chelmer Court
Church Street
Chelmsford CM1 1NH
Tel: 0245 492385
Tlx: 995910

Reigate (area office for Kent, West Sussex, East Sussex and Surrey)

Douglas House
London Road
Reigate RH2 9QP
Tel: 0737 226900
Tlx: 918364 DTIRGT G
Fax: 0737 223491

East Kent (satellite office)

The Old Town Hall
Market Street
Margate CT9 1EU
Tel: 0843 290511

Chatham (satellite office)

Kent Export Centre Ltd
The Gatehouse
St George's Centre
Chatham Maritime
Gillingham ME4 4UH
Tel: 0634 829299
Fax: 0634 829425

Northwest

Sunley Tower
Piccadilly Plaza
Manchester M1 4BA
Tel: 061 236 2171
Tlx: 667104
Fax: 061 228 3740

Liverpool (this office covers Liverpool, Widnes–Runcorn and Wirral–Chester)

Graeme House
Derby Square
Liverpool L2 7UP
Tel: 051 227 4111
Tlx: 627647 DTILPLUG
Fax: 051 236 1140
Merlintex: 944-512
    363079 DTILIV

DTI Northwest (satellite offices)

Cheshire Office
Scope House
Weston Road
Crewe CW1 1DD
Tel: 0270 500706 (direct line)
Fax: 0270 582506

Lancashire Office
Chamber of Commerce House
2 Camden Place
Preston   PR1 8BE
Tel: 0772 204134 (direct line)
        0772 555246 (switchboard)
Tlx: 677467 CHACOMG
Fax: 0772 201184

Cumbria Office
Kendal College
Milnthorpe Road
Kendal   LA9 5AY
Tel: 0539 23067 (direct line)
Fax: 0539 27804

The following act as DTI regional offices:
Scottish office

Alhambra House
45 Waterloo Street
Glasgow   G2 6AT
Tel: 041 242 2855
Tlx: 777883
Fax: 041 248 2855 ext. 347

Welsh Office

New Crown Building
Cathays Park
Cardiff   CF1 3NQ
Tel: 0222 825111
Tlx: 498228
Fax: 0222 823088

**Industrial Development
Board for Northern Ireland**

IDB House
64 Chichester Street
Belfast   BT1 4JX
Tel: 0232 233233
Tlx: 747 025
Fax: 0232 231328

Appendix 4: Department of Trade and Industry country desks

All information on trade with foreign countries may be obtained from

Department of Trade and Industry
1 Victoria Street
London   SW1H 0ET
Tel: 01 215 7877

The following table supplies the telephone numbers for information on each country. Callers should dial 01 215 followed by the four-figure number given.

Country	Room	Extension	Country	Room	Extension
Afghanistan	137	4367/4395[a]	Bhutan	307	4825
Albania	316	4734	Bolivia	105	5288
Algeria	112	4947/4948	Botswana	157	5011/5274[a]
Andorra	356	4357/4284[a]4260	Brazil	105	5293/5051[a]
		4768	British Indian	142	4971
Angola	157	5018	Ocean		4974[a]
		5023	Territories		
Anguilla	123	5297/5040[a]	(BOIT)		
Antigua	123	5297/5040[a]	Brunei	341	5143/5465[a]
Argentina	101	5055	Bulgaria	316	4734
Ascension Island	157	5018/5023	Burkina Faso	145	5034/5035[a]
Australia	119	5318/5321[a]	Burma	320	4738/4741[a]
		5319[a]	Burundi	142	4971/4974[a]
Austria	361	4798/5179[a]	Cameroon	142	4971/4973[a]
Azores	356	5307			4974[a]
Bahamas	123	5297/5040[a]	Canada		
Bahrain	130	5221	Consumer goods	558	5327/
Bangladesh	307	4824/4821[a]	Capital goods	556	4593[a]/4595[a]
Barbados	123	5297/5040[a]		502	4608/4605[a]
Belgium	371	5486/4794		557	5185[a]/4663[a]
Bellze	123	5297/5040[a]	Canary Islands	356	4357/4284[a]/4260
Benin	145	5034	Cape Verde	145	5034/5035[a]
		5035[a]	Cayman Islands	123	5297/5040[a]
Bermuda	556	4594[a]	Central	142	4973

[a] Tariff and import regulation enquiries only.

Country	Room	Extension	Country	Room	Extension
African Republic		4974[a]	Germany (GDR)	335	5267/5152
Chad	145	5034/5035[a]	Chana	138	4969/4970[a]
Chile	101	5383	Gibraltar	356	4284/4260/5307
China	309	5252/4829	Greece		
Colombia	105	5289/5490[a]	Consumer goods	362	5103
Comoros	142	4971	Capital goods		4776
Congo	142	4973/4974[a]	Grenada	123	5297/5040[a]
Costa Rica	129	5036/5035[a]	Guadeloupe	123	5297/5451[a]
Cote d'Ivoire	145	5034/5035	Guatemala	129	5036
Cuba	129	5036/	Guinea	145	5034/5035[a]
	123[a]	5296[a]	Guinea Bissau	145	5034/5035[a]
Cyprus	110	5358			5296[a]
Czechoslovakia	335	5267/5152	Haiti	123	5297/5040[a]
Denmark	376	5341/4397	Honduras	129	5036
		5140	Hong Kong	309	4828/4830
Djibouti	136	4965	Hungary	316	4734
Dominica	123	5297/5040[a]	Iceland	376	4783/5134[a]
Dominician	129	5036	India	307	4825
Republic			Indo-China	320	4736/4737[a]
Ecuador	105	5288	Indonesia	320	4738/4741[a]
Egypt	104	4947/4948[a]	Iran	137	4367/4395[a]
El Salvador	129	5036	Iraq	139A	4367/4395[a]
Equatorial	142	4973	Ireland	376	4783/5134[a]
Guinea		4974[a]	Israel	110	4949/4240[a]
Ethiopia	136	4965	Italy		
Falkland Islands	101	5055	Consumer goods	362	5103
Fiji	119	4759/4760[a]	Capital goods		4776[a]
Finland	376	4783/5134[a]	Jamaica	123	5297/5040[a]
France			Japan	353	4804/4805[a]
Consumer goods	350	4765/4762	Jordan	137	5169/5314[a]
Capital goods	352	5451/5197	Kampuchea	320	4736/4737[a]
French Guiana	123	5297/5451[a]	Kenya	136	5226
French Polynesia	119	4759/4760[a]	Kiribati	119	4759/4760[a]
French West Indies	123	5297/5461[a]	Korea, South	336	4747/4809[a]
Gabon	142	4973/4974[a]	Korea, North	320	4736/4737[a]
Gambia	138	4969/4970[a]	Kuwait	130	5081
Germany (FRG)			Laos	320	4736/4737[a]
Consumer goods and all general inquiries including regulations and tariffs	363	4796	Lebanon	139A	5169/5314[a]
			Lesotho	157	5011/5274[a]
			Liberia	138	4969/4970[a]
			Libya	110	5358
			Liechtenstein	363	4359
			Luxembourg	371	5486/4794[a]
Capital goods – market info. only	361	5179	Macao	309	4828/5273/4829

[a] Tariff and import regulation enquiries only.

153

Country	Room	Extension
Madagascar	142	4971
		4974[a]
Madeira	356	5307
Malawi	157	5018/5023[a]
Malaysia	341	5143/5465[a]
Maldives	307	4825
Mali	145	5034/5035[a]
Malta	110	5358
Marshall Islands	119	4759/4760[a]
Martinique	123	5297/5451[a]
Mauritania	145	5034/5035[a]
Mauritius	142	4971
Mayotte	142	4971
Mexico	129	5290/4297[a]
Monaco	350	4762
Mongolia	327	4734
Montserrat	123	5297/5040[a]
Morocco	104	4947
Namibia		
Capital goods	157	5011/5274[a]
Consumer goods	157	4308/5274[a]
Nepal	307	4821/4824[a]
Netherlands	371	4790/5486[a]
Netherlands	123	5297/5040[a]
Antilles		
New Caledonia	119	4759/4760[a]
New Zealand	119	4759/4760[a]
		4398[a]
Nicaragua	129	5036
Niger	145	5034/5035[a]
Nigeria	138	4967/4968[a]
Norway	376	5341/4397
		5140
Oman	130	5081
Pacific Islands	119	4759/4760[a]
Pakistan	307	4821/4824[a]
Panama	129	5036
Papua New Guinea	119	4759/4760[a]
Paraguay	101	5383
Peru	105	5288
Phillippines	341	5253/5489[a]
Poland	316	4734
Portugal	356	4357/5307[a]
Puerto Rico	123	5297/4607
Qatar	130	4246/5221[a]

Country	Room	Extension
Réunion	142	4971/4974[a]
Romania	335	5267/5152
Rwanda	142	4971/4974[a]
San Marino	362	5103/4776[a]
Sao Tome	157	5018/5023
and Principe		
St Helena	157	5018/5023
St Kitts/Nevis	123	5297/5040[a]
St Lucia	123	5297/5040[a]
St Vincent	123	5297/5040[a]
Saudi Arabia	130	5239/4362[a]
		5052[a]
Senegal	145	5034/5035[a]
Seychelles	142	4973/4974[a]
Sierra Leone	138	4969/4970[a]
Singapore	341	5143/5465[a]
Solomon	119	4759/4760[a]
Islands		
Somalia	136	4965
South Africa		
Capital goods	157	5011/5274[a]
Consumer goods	157	4308/5274[a]
Spain		
Capital goods	356	4357
Consumer goods	356	4768
		4284[a]/4260[a]/
		5307
Sri Lanka	307	4825/4826[a]
Sudan	110	5358
Suriname	123	5297/5296[a]
Swaziland	157	5011/5274[a]
Sweden	376	5341/4397/514€
Switzerland	363	4359/5245[a]
Syria	137	4367/4305[a]
Taiwan	309	4729/4830[a]
Tanzania	136	5226
Thailand	341	5253/5489[a]
Togo	145	5034/5035[a]
Tonga	119	4759/4760[a]
Trinidad and	123	5297/5296[a]
Tabago		
Tristan Da	157	5018/5023[a]
Cunha		
Tunisia	104	4947
Turkey	139A	5169/5134[a]

[a] Tariff and import regulation enquiries only.

Country	Room	Extension	Country	Room	Extension
Turks & Caicos	123	5297/5040[a]	Virgin Islands (USA)	123	5297/4606[a]
Tuvalu	119	4759/4760[a]	Western Sahara	145	5034/5035[a]
Uganda	136	4965	Western Samoa	119	4759/4760[a]
United Arab Emirates	130	4246/5221[a]	Yemen Arab Republic	130	4961/5096[a]
United States of America			Yemen Peoples Democratic Republic	130	4961/5096[a]
Consumer goods	556	4595/4593[a]	Yugoslavia	335	5267/5152
Capital goods	562	4605/4608[a]	Zaire	142	4973/4974[a]
	557	5185/4563[a]	Zambia	157	5018/5023[a]
Uruguay	101	5055	Zimbabwe	157	5018/5023[a]
USSR	331	5265			
Venezuela	105	5289/5490[a]			
Vietnam	320	4736/4737[a]			
Virgin Islands (British)	123	5297/5040[a]			

[a] Tariff and import regulation enquiries only.

Appendix 5: Simpler Trade Procedures Board services

SITPRO
Venture House
29 Glasshouse St
London W1R 5RG
Tel: 01 287 3525

Spex 3

ESL Computer Services Ltd
Beckenham
Tel: 01 658 7821

International Software
    Marketing Ltd
East Grinstead
Tel: 0342 324117

Nord Systems Ltd
Leeds
Tel: 0532 444577

The Software Connection Ltd
Fareham
Tel: 0329 221066

XEROX Design Technology
Uxbridge
Tel: 0895 441693

Interbridge 4

SD SCICON PLC
Cheadle
Tel: 061 428 0811

ESL Computer Services Ltd
Beckenham
Tel: 01 658 7821

The Software Connection Ltd
Fareham
Tel: 0329 221066

Hoskyns Group Plc
Birmingham
Tel: 021 333 3536

Stationery products

Formecon Services Ltd
Crewe
Tel: 0270 500800

J A Oldham (Printers Ltd)
Huddersfield
Tel: 0484 530789

Lonsdale Business Forms Ltd
Wellingborough
Tel: 0933 228855

LT Printing
Birkenhead
Tel: 051 647 8006

Nationwide Business Forms Ltd
St Austell
Tel: 0726 72548

Systemforms Ltd
Woodford Green
Tel: 01 505 6125

Tate Freight Forms
Milton Keynes
Tel: 0908 567687

Copier systems

ALS Freight Services
Stoke-on-Trent
Tel: 0782 208777

Export Advisory Services
Beccles
Tel: 0502 717877

Export Analysis Ltd
Leamington Spa
Tel: 0926 311537

Export Development Associates
Colne
Tel: 0282 815697

Export Development Services
Southampton
Tel: 0703 332787

Export Paperwork Services Ltd
Stansted Airport
Tel: 0279 871010

Export Trade Connections
Daventry
Tel: 0327 705392

Impex Advisory Services
Symington
Tel: 0563 830239

Maclean Systems Ltd
Glasgow
Tel: 041 649 3710

Maxwell Terence Ltd
Hereford
Tel: 0432 277711

Newman White Ltd
Trowbridge
Tel: 02214 62337

Northern Export Systems Supplies
South Wirral
Tel: 051 336 7080

P & H Export Services Ltd
Ashton-under-Lyne
Tel: 061 339 0821

Playle Reprographics Ltd
Clacton-on-Sea
Tel: 0255 426342

Appendix 6: International fund agencies for economic development in developing countries

List of agencies

Agency Name	*Agency Code*
Abu Dhabi Fund for Arab Economic Development	ADFAED
African Development Bank Group	AFDBG
Arab Bank for Economic Development in Africa	BADEA
Arab Fund for Economic and Social Development	AFESD
Asian Development Bank	ADB
Caribbean Development Bank	CDB
Centre for Industrial Development	CID
European Economic Community	EEC
European Investment Bank	EIB
Inter-American Development Bank	IDB
International Fund for Agricultural Development	IFAD
Iraqui Fund for External Development	IFED
Islamic Development Bank	ISDB
Kuwait Fund for Arab Economic Development	KFAED
OPEC Fund for International Development	OPECF
Saudi Fund for Development	SFD
UN (UN agencies not otherwise specified)	UN
UN Industrial Development Organization	UNIDO
United Nations Development Programme	UNDP
World Bank Group	WBG

Key addresses

The World Bank (London office)
New Zealand House
Haymarket
London   SW1Y 4TE
Tel: 01 930 8511

European Commission
Director General VIII (Development)
200 rue de la Loi
B1049 Brussels
Tel: 010 322 235 1111

World Aid Section
Dept of Trade and Industry
1 Victoria Street
London   SW1H 0ET
Tel: 01 215 5369/4372

Appendix 7: British Chambers of Commerce export services and other sources of export advice

All the Chambers of Commerce in the table below provide the following services:

issue of certificates of origin
certification and authentication of signatures on export documents
conferences and seminars

The following Chambers of Commerce also have export advisers:

Bristol   0272 737373
Dorset   0202 682000
Leicester   0533 471237
Yorkshire and Humberside   0924 290525

The following other organizations have export advisers:

Essex Export Enterprise Centre, Chelmsford   0245 283030
Federation of Sussex Industries, Gatwick   0293 560884
Dover Export and Trade Centre   0304 241020
Kent Export Centre, Chatham   0634 828688

The following abbreviations are used in the table below:

C – ATA carnets
A – Arab states certificate of origin
T – trade missions
L – language and translation
E – active exporting advisers
O – on-line export information
B – BC-Net
N – trade bulletins
I – European information centre

Chamber	Tel.	C	A	T	L	E	O	B	N	I
Aberdeen	0224 641222				L	E	O		N	
Barnsley	0226 201166				L				N	
Birmingham	021 454 6171	C	A	T	L	E	O	B	N	I
Blackburn	0254 664747			T	L				N	
Bolton	0204 33896				L				N	
Boston and district	0205 51144									
Bradford	0274 728166		A	T	L		O		N	
Burnley	0282 36555				L					
Burton-upon-Trent and district	0283 63761				L		O			
Bury and district	061 764 8640									
Calderdale	0422 345631									
Cambridge and district	0223 7414		A		L				N	
Cardiff	0222 481648		A	T	L	E	O	B	N	
Carlisle	0288 26288									
Central and West Lancashire										
Central Scotland	0234 716868		A		L				N	
Chester and North Wales	0244 311704				L					
Chesterfield and North Derbyshire	0246 203456			T	L				N	
Colchester	0206 765279		A						N	
Coventry	0203 633000		A	T	L	E	O		N	
Derby and Derbyshire	0322 47031			T	L		O		N	
Doncaster	0302 341000				L				N	
Dudley	0384 237653									
Edinburgh	031 225 5851	C	A	T	L	E	O	B	N	
Exeter and district	0392 436641/2			T		E	O		N	
Fareham	0329 82250									
Fife	0592 201932				L					
Glasgow	041 204 2121	C	A	T	L	E	O		N	
Goole	0405 69164				L	E				
Grantham	0436 66661									
Greenock	0475 83678				L				N	
Grimsby and Immingham	0472 42981								N	
Guernsey	0481 27483									
Guildford and district	0483 37449				L					
Halton	09285 60958									
Hertfordshire	07072 72771/3	C	A		L		O			
Hull	0482 24976		A	T	L				N	

Appendix 7: British Chambers of Commerce export services

Chamber	Tel.	\<Services offered\>								
		C	A	T	L	E	O	B	N	I
Ipswich and Suffolk	0473 210611		A	T	L				N	
Isle of Man	0624 74941									
Isle of Wight	0983 524390									
Jersey	0534 24536/ 71031									
Kendal	0539 720049/ 7221122									
Kidderminster	0562 515515/ 744937			T	L				N	
Lancaster	0524 39467				L					
Leeds	0532 430491	C	A	T	L				N	
Lincoln	0522 523713				L					
London	01 248 4444	C	A	T		E	O	B	N	
Lowestoft	0502 569383				L					
Luton, Bedford and district	0582 23456/ 416943		A	T		E			N	
Manchester	061 2363210	C	A	T		E	O	B	N	I
Medway and Gillingham	0634 830001		A	T					N	
Merseyside	051 2271234	C	A	T	L	E	O	B	N	I
Newark	0636 640555									
Newhaven	0273 513307									
Newport and Gwent	0633 256093				L				N	
Northamptonshire	0604 22422		A	T	L					
Northern Ireland	0232 24413	C	A	T		E		B	N	
North Staffordshire	0782 202222		A	T	L				N	
Norwich and Norfolk	0603 625977/ 625992			T	L	E	O			I
Nottinghamshire	0602 624624	C	A	T	L	E	O	B	N	I
Oldham and district	061 6242482								N	
Oxford and district	0865 792020				L					
Paisley	041 8899291			T						
Perthshire	0738 37626									
Peterborough	0733 42658								N	
Plymouth	0752 221151			T	L		O		N	
Port Talbot	0792 71505									
Reading and Central Berkshire	0734 59049		A		L	E		B	N	I
Redditch	0527 67692		A		L					
Rochdale	0706 343810				L				N	
Royal Turnbridge Wells	0892 546888				L					

Appendix 7: British Chambers of Commerce export services

Chamber	Tel.	Services offered								
		C	A	T	L	E	O	B	N	I
Rugby and district	0788 544951				L					
Sandwell	021 5532821				L				N	
Scunthrope, Glandford and Gainsborough	0724 841209				L					
Sheffield	0742 766667		A	T	L		O	B	N	
Shropshire	0952 588766		A		L				N	I
Southend on Sea and district	0702 77090/ 78380				L				N	
Southeast Hampshire	0705 294111	C	A	T	L	E	O	B		
South of Scotland	0450 72267									
Swansea	0792 653297/8									
Teeside and district	0642 230023					E	O		N	
Thames and Chilterns	0753 77877		A	T	L	E	O	B	N	
Tyne and Wear	091 261 1142		A		L	E	O		N	
Walsall	0922 721777		A	T	L				N	
Warrington	0925 35054				L		O			
Westminster	01 7342851		A	T	L			B	N	
Wigan and district	0942 496047				L		O		N	
Wolverhampton	0902 26726		A	T	L	E	O		N	
Worcester and Hereford	0905 611611/2			T	L	E			N	

Other affiliated Chambers (not licenced to issue certs of origin)

Chamber	Tel.
Inverness and district	0463 233570
Leith	031 2255851
Neath, Briton Ferry	0639 820269
Rotherham	0909 362001
St Helens	0744 613068/ 629861
Salford	061 2363210
Tynedale	0434 607354/ 603164
York	0904 629513

Appendix 8: Overseas country Chambers of Commerce in the UK

American Chamber of Commerce
(UK)
75 Brook Street
London   W1Y 2EB
Tel: 01 493 0381
Tlx: 23675 ANCHANG G

Anglo-Zaire Chamber of Commerce
43 Chase Side
Southgate
London   N14 5BP
Tel: 01 882 1197
Tlx: 264901 LITGET G
Fax: 01 882 7423

Arab–British Chamber of Commerce
6 Belgrave Square
London   SW1X 8PH
Tel: 01 235 4363
Tlx: 299484 ARABIS G
Fax: 01 245 6688

Australian–British Chamber of
Commerce (UK)
Suite 615, 6th Floor,
Linen Hall
162–8 Regent Street
London   W1R 5TB
Tel: 01 439 0086
Tlx: 268312 WESCOM G
      (attention AUSTNZ)
Fax: 01 734 0670
      (attention AUSTNZ)

Belgo-Luxembourg Chamber of
Commerce in Great Britain
6 John Street
London   WC1N 2ES
Tel: 01 831 3508
Tlx: 23467 TAWLON G
Fax: 01 831 9151

Brazilian Chamber of Commerce
in Great Britain
32 Green Street
London   W1Y 4AT
Tel: 01 499 0186
Tlx: 25814 BRASTIC

British–American Chamber of
Commerce
Suite 305
19 Stratford Place
London   W1N 9AF
Tel: 01 491 3361
Tlx: 291429 NETNYN G
Fax: 01 493 8280

British–Israel Chamber of
Commerce
14–15 Rodmarton Street
London   W1H 3FW
Tel: 01 486 2371/4
Tlx: 267141
Fax: 01 487 2679

British–Soviet Chamber of
  Commerce
60A Pembroke Road
London W8 6NX
Tel: 01 602 7692
Tlx: 8813515
Fax: 01 371 4788

Canada–United Kingdom Chamber
  Of Commerce
British Columbia House
3 Regent Street
London SQ1Y 4NZ
Tel: 01 930 7711/3
Tlx: 917369
Fax: 01 930 2012

Chinese Chamber of Commerce
  (UK)
20 Frith Street
London W1
Tel: 01 734 5984/6502

Egyptian–British Chamber of
  Commerce
4 Kent House
Market Place
London W1A 4EG
Tel: 01 323 2856
Tlx: 22581 EGBRIT G
    PO Box 4EG

French Chamber of Commerce
  in Great Britain
Knightsbridge House
2nd Floor
197 Knightsbridge
London SW7 1RB
Tel: 01 225 5250
Tlx: 269132 SACROM G
Fax: 01 225 5557

German Chamber of Industry and
  Commerce in the UK
12–13 Suffolk Street
St James's
London SW1Y 4HG
Tel: 01 930 7251
Tlx: 919442 GERMAN G
Fax: 01 930 2726

Indian Chamber of Commerce
  in Great Britain
124 Middlesex Street
London E1 7HY
Tel: 01 247 8078

Italian Chamber of Commerce
  for Great Britain
Walmar House
296 Regent Street
London W1R 6AE
Tel: 01 637 3153/3062
Tlx: 296096 ITACAM
Fax: 01 436 6037

Japanese Chamber of Commerce
  and Industry in the UK
5th Floor
Chronicle House
.72–8 Fleet Street
London EC4Y 1HY
Tel: 01 353 8166/5977

Mauritius Chamber of Agriculture
Grosvenor Garden House
35–7 Grosvenor Gardens
London SW1W OBS
Tel: 01 834 3381/01 828 5363
Tlx: 267661

Netherlands–British Chamber
of Commerce
The Dutch House
307–8 High Holborn
London   WC1V 7LS
Tel: 01 405 1358
Tlx: 23211
Fax: 01 405 1689

New Zealand–United Kingdom
Chamber of Commerce and
Industry
Suite 615, 6th Floor
Linen Hall
162–8 Regent Street
London   W1R 5TB
Tel: 01 439 0086
Tlx: 268312 WESCOM G
(attention AUSTNZ)
Fax: 01 734 0670
(attention AUSTNZ)

Nigerian–British Chamber of
Commerce
registered office: Brittingham House
Orchard Street
Crawley
West Sussex
London   RH11 7AE
Tel: 0435 872128

replies: The Executive Secretary
PO Box 118
Mayfield
East Sussex   TN20 6BQ

Norwegian Chamber of Commerce
London Incorporated
Norway House
21–4 Cockspur Street
London   SW1Y 5BN
Tel: 01 930 0181/2
Tlx: 917294 NORCC G
Fax: 01 930 3992

Papua New Guinea–United
Kingdom Chamber of Commerce
and Industry
Suite 615, 6th Floor
Linen Hall
162–8 Regent Street
London   W1R 5TB
Tel: 01 439 0086
Tlx: 268312 WESCOM G

Portuguese Chamber of Commerce
and Industry in the UK
4th Floor
New Bond Street House
1–5 New Bond Street
London   W1Y 9PE
Tel: 01 493 9973
Tlx: 918089
Fax: 01 493 4772

Spanish Chamber of Commerce in
Great Britain
5 Cavendish Square
London   W1M ODP
Tel: 01 637 9061
Tlx: 8811583

Swedish Chamber of Commerce
for the United Kingdom
72–3 Welbeck Street
London   W1M 7HA
Tel: 01 486 4545
Tlx:2260 SWETRA G
Fax: 01 935 5487

Turkish–British Chamber of
Commerce
2nd Floor
Avon House
360–6 Oxford Street
London   W1N 9HA
Tel: 01 491 4636/01 499 4265
Tlx: 28800 LONDOF G
Fax: 01 493 5548
(attention TBCCI)

Yugoslavia Chamber of Economy
Crown House
143–7 Regent Street
London   W1R 7LB
Tel: 01 734 2581
Tlx: 27552

UK–Caribbean Chamber of
Commerce
99 Stoke Newington Church Street
London   N16 OUD
Tel: 01 254 4532

UK–Pakistan Overseas Chambers
of Commerce and Industry
5 Bathurst Street
London   W2 2SD
Tel: 01 262 7599

Appendix 9: Continental section of British Chambers of Commerce

British Trade Council in Austria
Mollwald Platz 1/12
A-1040 Vienna
Tel: 010 43 222 65 43 63

British Chamber of Commerce for
  Belgium and Luxembourg
30 rue Joseph II
B 1040 Brussels
Tel: 010 32 2 219 07 88

British Import Union in Denmark
Borsbygningen
DK-127 Copenhagen K
Tel: 010 451 13 6349

Franco-British Chamber of
  Commerce and Industry
8 rue Cimarosa
F 75116 Paris
Tel: 010 331 45 051308

British Chamber of Commerce
  in Germany
Heumart 14
5000 Koln
Tel: 010 49 221 234284/5

British Hellenic Chamber of
  Commerce
4 Valaoritu
Athens GR 10671
Tel: 010 30 1 72 10 361

The British Chamber of Commerce
  in Italy
via Agnello 8
20121 Milan
Tel: 010 39 2 876981

Netherland–British Chamber of
  Commerce
Holland Trade House
Bezuidenhoutseweg 181
2594 AH, The Hague
Tel: 010 441 405 1358

British–Portuguese Chamber of
  Commerce (Camarade Comercio
  Luso Britanica)
Rua da Estrela 8
P 1200 Lisbon
Tel: 010 351 1 661586

British Chamber of Commerce in
  Spain
Plaza de Santa Barbara 10
28004 Madrid
Tel: 010 34 1 30830

The British–Swiss Chamber of
  Commerce
155 Freiestrasse
CH 8032 Zurich
Tel: 010 41 1 553131

The British Chamber of Commerce
  in Turkey
PO Box 190 Karakoy
Istanbul
Tel: 010 90 1 1490658

Appendix 10: Language export centres

National LX Co-ordinator
Language-Export Ltd
PO Box 1574
Regents College
Inner Circle
Regents Park
London   NW1 4NJ
Tel: 01 224 3748
Fax: 01 224 3518

Coventry LX Centre
Coventry Technical College
Butts
Coventry   CV1 3GD
Tel: 0203 256793
Fax: 0203 520164

East Anglian LX Centre
EARCB
2 Looms Lane
Bury St Edmunds
Suffolk   IP33 1HB
Tel: 0284 764977

East Midlands Languages for
  Exporters
EMLEX
LISU University of Technology
Loughborough   LE11 3TU
Tel: 0509 222386
Fax: 0509 610361

International Business and Export
  Services (IBEX)
HAPSU
Education Department
The Castle
Winchester   SO23 8UG
Tel: 0962 846285
Fax: 0962 846456

IC (Languages and Communication
  Services) Ltd
Aston Science Park
Love Lane
Aston
Birmingham   B47 4BJ
Tel: 021 359 0981

Lancashire and Cumbria LX Centre
Lancashire Polytechnic
Preston
Lancashire   PR1 2TQ
Tel: 0772 201201 ext. 2232/
    0772 262002
Fax: 0772 202073

Language Consultants for Industry
14 Queen Square
Bath   BA1 2HH
Tel: 0225 24929

London Language-Export Centre
(LEXCEL)
3rd Floor
72 Great Portland Street
London   W1N 5AL
Tel: 01 323 4977

London Language-Export Centre
(South)
School of Languages
Kingston Polytechnic
Penrhyn Road
Kingston upon Thames
Surrey   KT1 2EE
Tel: 01 549 1366 ext. 2289
Fax: 01 547 1277

Manchester Languages Consortium
Room 613
All Saints Building
Manchester Polytechnic
All Saints
Manchester   M15 6BH
Tel: 061 228 6171 ext. 2170

Merseyside Language Export Centre
Modern Languages Building
Room 405
University of Liverpool
Liverpool   L69 3BX
Tel: 051 794 2796

North East Export Associates
(NEEXA)
Room B218
Newcastle Polytechnic
Ellison Building
Ellison Place
Newcastle upon Tyne   NE1 8ST
Tel: 091 261 0190

Oxford and Thames Valley Export
Centre
The Cricket Road Centre
Cricket Road
Oxford   OX4 3DW
Tel: 0865 747221

The Scottish LX Consortium
External Education Services Office
2 The Square
University of Glasgow
Glasgow   G12 8QQ
Tel: 041 339 4991/4987/4977

Services for Export and Language
(SEL)
Room 122
Crescent House
University of Salford
Salford   M5 4WT
Tel: 061 745 7480/061 736 5843
ext. 367

Staffordshire and Wolverhampton
Language-Export Centre (North)
The Management Centre
College Road
Stoke-on-Trent   ST4 2DE
Tel: 0782 412143

Staffordshire and Wolverhampton
Language-Export Centre (South)
School of Languages and European
Studies
Wolverhampton
Stafford Street
Wolverhampton   WV1 1SB
Tel: 0902 313001 ext. 2471
Fax: 0902 25015

Sussex and Kent LX Centre
The Language Centre
Brighton Polytechnic
Falmer
Brighton   BN1 9PH
Tel: 0273 606622

Wales Language and Export
   Training Centre
Science Tower
University College Swansea
Singleton Park
Swansea   SA2 8PP
Tel: 0792 295621

Wales Language and Export
   Training Centre (North)
Newtech Innovation Centre
Deeside Industrial Park
Deeside
Clwyd   CH5 2NU
Tel: 0244 822881
Tlx: 617134 NEWTEC
Fax: 0244 822002

Yorkshire and Humberside Export
   Services (YES)
26 Springfield Mount
Leeds   LS2 9ND
Tel: 0532 455204

Appendix 11: Professional institutes

Institute of Credit Management
Easton House
Easton on the Hill
Stamford   PE9 3NH
Tel: 0780 56777
Tlx: 32251

Institute of Commerce
64 Clifton Street
London   EC2A 4HB
Tel: 01 247 9812

Institute of Export
64 Clifton Street
London   EC2A 4HB
Tel: 01 247 9812

Institute of Freight Forwarders
Redfern House
Browells Lane
Feltham
Middlesex   TW13 7EP
Tel: 01 844 2266
Tlx: 8953060
Fax: 01 890 5546

Institute of Logistics and
   Distribution Management
Douglas House
Corby   NN17 1PL
Tel: 0536 205500

The Chartered Institute of
   Marketing
Moor Hall
Cookham
Maidenhead
Berkshire   SL6 9QH
Tel: 06285 24922
Tlx: 849462 TELEFAC G
Fax: 06285 31382

Institute of Packaging
Sysonby Lodge
Nottingham Road
Melton Mowbray
Leicestershire   LE13 0NV
Tel: 0664 500055

Institute of Chartered
   Shipbrokers
24 St Mary Axe
London   EC3A 8DE
Tel: 01 283 1361

Institute of Transport
   Administration
32 Palmerston Road
Southampton SO1 1LL
Tel: 0703 631380

Chartered Institute of
   Transport (CIT)
80 Portland Place
London   W1N 4DP
Tel: 01 636 9952

Appendix 12: On-line databases and information providers

Export Network Ltd
Regency House
1–4 Warwick Street
London   W1R 5WA
Tel: 01 494 4030
Fax: 01 494 1245

Helpline Databases
Helpline Information Service
British Institute of Management
Management House
Cottingham Road
Northants   NN17 1TT
Tel: 0536 204222
Fax: 0536 201651

Kompass Online
Reed Information Services Ltd
East Grinstead House
East Grinstead
West Sussex   RH19 1XA
Tel: 0342 326972
Tlx: 95127 INFSER G

Pergamon Financial Data Services
Achilles House
Western Avenue
London   W3 OUA
Tel: 01 992 3456
Tlx: 8814614
Fax: 01 993 7335

Predicaste Europe
8–10 Denman Street
London   W1V PRF
Tel: 01 494 3817
Fax: 01 734 5938

Dialog Information Retrieval
   Services
PO Box 188
Oxford   OX1 5AX
Tel: 0865 730275

Data-Star
Plaza Suite
114 Jermyn Street
London   SW1Y 6HJ
Tel: 01 930 5503

Profile Information
Financial Times Business
   Information (FTBI)
Sunbury House
79 Staines Road West
Sunbury-on-Thames
Middlesex   TW16 7AH
Tel: 0932 761444
Fax: 0932 781452

Barclays Bank plc
Trade Development Service
International Trade Services
   Department
Fleetway House
25 Farringdon Street
London   EC4A 4LT
Tel: 01 489 0969

Appendix 13: Useful addresses

General

Association of British Factors Ltd
Hind Court
147 Fleet Street
London   EC4A 2BV
Tel: 01 353 1213
Tlx: 298681

British Exporters Association
16 Dartmouth Street
London   SW1H 9BL
Tel: 01 222 5419
Tlx: 8814718 EEFBH G
      attention BEHA
Fax: 01 222 2782

British Franchise Association Ltd
75a Bell Street
Henley on Thames
Oxon   RG9 2BD
Tel: 0491 578049/50

British Importers Confederation
69 Cannon Street
London   EC4N 5AB
Tel: 01 248 4444

British Invisible Exports Council
  (BIEC)
Windsor House
39 King Street
London   EC2V 8DQ
Tel: 01 600 1198
Tlx: 9413342 BIE G
Fax: 01 606 4248

Bill of Entry Service
Statistics Office
Portcullis House
27 Victoria Avenue
Southend-on-Sea   SS2 6AL
Tel: 0702 49421

CCN Business Information Ltd
Abbey House
Abbeyfield Road
Lenton
Nottingham   NG7 2SW
Tel: 0602 863864
Tlx: 37663
Fax: 0602 483436

The Centre for International Briefing
The Castle
Farnham
Surrey   GV9 OAG
Tel: 0252 721194

Chemical Industries
  Association Ltd
Kings Buildings
Smith Square
London   SW1P 3JJ
Tel: 01 834 3399
Tlx: 916672
Fax: 01 834 4469

Commission of the
  European Communities
8 Storey's Gate
London   SW1P 3AT
Tel: 01 222 8122
Tlx: 23208 EUR UKG
Fax: 01 222 0900

Confederation of British
  Industry (CBI)
Centre Point
103 New Oxford Street
London   WC1A 1DU
Tel: 01 379 7400
Fax: 01 240 1578

Consumer Affairs (Marking
  of Goods)
Fair Trading Division
Department of Trade and
  Industry
Millbank Tower
London   SW1P 4QU
Tel: 01 211 3204

Cooperative Development
  Agency
Broadmead House
21 Panton Street
London   SW1Y 4DR
Tel: 01 839 2988

HM Customs and Excise HQ
Kings Beam House
Mark Lane
London   EC3R 7HE
Tel: 01 626 1515
Fax: 01 382 5570

HM Customs and Excise
General Enquiries
New Kings Beam House
22 Upper Ground
London SE1 9PS
Tel: 01 620 1313

Defence Sales Organisation
Ministry of Defence
Stuart House
23–5 Soho Square
London   W1V 5FJ
Tel: 01 632 4826

The Design Council
28 Haymarket
London SW1Y 4SU
Tel: 01 839 8000
Fax: 01 925 2130

The Developing Countries Trade
  Agency
69 Cannon Street
London   EC4N 5AB
Tel: 01 248 4444

Direct Mail Producers Association
  (DMPA)
34 Grand Avenue
London   N10 3BP
Tel: 01 883 9854/5

Direct Mail Services Standards
  Board
26 Eccleston Street
London   SW1W 9PY
Tel: 01 824 8651

Dunn & Bradstreet plc
26–32 Clifton Street
London   EC2P 2LY
Tel: 01 377 4377
Tlx: 886697
Fax: 01 247 3836

Duty Remissions Branch
Department of Trade and Industry
Kingsgate House
1 Victoria Street
London   SW1E OET
Tel: 01 215 7877

Employment Conditions Abroad Ltd
   (ECA)
Anchor House
15 Britten Street
London   SW3 3TY
Tel: 01 351 7151
Tlx: 299751 EURECA G
Fax: 01 351 9396

Export Buying Offices Association
c/o Portman Ltd
360 Oxford Street
London   W1A 4BX
Tel: 01 493 8141
Tlx: 263929 PORTMAN G
Fax: 01 499 2134

Export Licensing Unit
Department of Trade and Industry
Kingsgate House
66–74 Victoria Street
London   SW1E 6SW
Tel: 01 215 8070/8376

Export Marketing Research Scheme
The Association of British Chambers
   of Commerce
4 Westwood House
Westwood Business Park
Coventry   CV4 8HS
Tel: 0203 694484
Fax: 0203 694690

Export Opportunities Ltd
Export House
87a Wembley Hill Road
Wembley
Middlesex   HA9 8BU
Tel: 01 900 1313
Fax: 01 900 1268

Fairs & Promotions Branch
Dept of Trade and Industry
Dean Bradley House
Horseferry Road
London   SW1P 2AG
Tel: 01 276 3000

Graydon-ATP International Ltd
Hyde House
Edgeware Road
Colindale
London   NW9 6LW
Tel: 01 975 1050
Tlx: 21632/261203
Fax: 01 975 1099

Henley Distance Learning Ltd
Greenlands
Henley on Thames
Oxon   RG9 3AU
Tel: 0491 571552
Tlx: 847071 HOMED G
Fax: 0491 57943

ICI Tradeway
ICI College House
Great Portland Street
London   SW1P 3JC
Tel: 01 834 4444
Tlx: 21324
Fax: 01 834 2042

Incorporated Society of British
   Advertisers (ISBA)
44 Hertford Street
London   W1Y 8AE
Tel: 01 499 7502
Tlx: 22525

Import Licensing Branch
Dept of Trade and Industry
Charles House
375 Kensington High Street
London   W14 8QH
Tel: 01 603 4444

JETRO (Japan External Trade
   Organization)
Leconfield House
Curzon Street
London   W1Y 7FB
Tel: 01 493 7226

Lloyds of London Press
Sheepen Place
Colchester
Essex   CO3 3LP
Tel: 0206 772277
Tlx: 987231 LLOYDS G
Fax: 0206 46273

London Chamber of Commerce
Marlowe House
Station Road
Sidcup
Kent   DA15 7BJ
Tel: 01 302 0261
Tlx: 888941 LCCI G
         (attention Exams Board)
Fax: 01 302 4169

National Council for Vocational
   Qualifications
222 Euston Road
London   NW1 2BZ
Tel: 01 387 9898
Fax: 01 387 0978

Royal Mail International Parcels
Freepost
Room 111
33 Grosvenor Place
London   SW1X 1EE
Tel: 01 245 7279
Fax: 01 235 0277

Sino-British Trade Council
Abford House
15 Wilton Road
London   SW1V 1LT
Tel: 01 828 5176

Small Firms & Tourism Division
Department of Employment
Room 121
Steel House
Tothill Street
London   SW1H 9NF
Tel: 01 273 4747

Tate Freight Forms
Tate Telex & Continuous
  Stationery Ltd
47 Burners Lane South
Kiln Farm
Milton Keynes MK11 3HD
Tel: 0908 567687
Tlx: 826932
Fax: 0908 564 622

Technical Help for Exporters
  (THE)
c/o British Standards Institute
Linford Wood
Milton Keynes MK14 6LE
Tel: 0908 220022
Tlx: 825777 BSIMK G
Fax: 0908 320856

Training Agency
Moorfoot
Sheffield S1 4PQ
Tel: 0742 753275
Fax: 0742 78316

Insurance and financing

Association of British Insurers
Aldermany House
Queen Street
London EC4N 1TT
Tel: 01 248 4477
Tlx: 937035

Barclays Bank plc
International Trade Services
  Department
Fleetway House
25 Farringdon Street
London EC4A 4LT
Tel: 01 489 0969

British Insurance Brokers
  Association
14 Bevis Marks
London EC3A 7NT
Tel: 01 623 9043
Tlx: 987321

CAD Consultants Ltd
797 London Road
Thornton Heath
Croydon
Surrey CR4 6XA
Tel: 01 684 2521

Export Credits Guarantee Dept
  (ECGD)
PO Box 272
50 Ludgate Hill
London EC4M 7AY
Tel: 01 382 7000/01 726 4050

The Export Finance Co Ltd
Exfinco House
Sanford Street
Swindon
Wiltshire SN1 1QQ
Tel: 0793 616333
Tlx: 444344 EXFIN G
Fax: 0793 614876

Trade Indemnity plc
12–34 Great Eastern Street
London EC2A 3AX
Tel: 01 739 4311
Tlx: 21227
Fax: 01 729 7682

Unicol Export Insurance Services
  Ltd
Chiltern House
54–6 High Street
Harrow-on-the-Hill
Middlesex HA1 3LL
Tel: 01 423 3355

Appendix 14: Inspection agencies

Cotecna International Ltd
Annabelle House
28 Staines Road
Hounslow
Middlesex   TN3 3JB
Tel: 01 577 6000
Tlx: 914013

Société Générale de Surveillance
(General Superintendance
Company)
SGS Inspection Services Ltd
SGS House
217–221 London Road
Camberley
Surrey   GU15 3EY
Tel: 0276 691133
Tlx: 858407   SGSCAM
Fax: 0276 691155

Crown Agents for Overseas
  Governments[1] & Administrations
St Nicholas House
St Nicholas Road
Sutton
Surrey
Tel: 01 643 3311
Tlx: 916205 CALOND G
Fax: 01 643 8232

Lloyd's Register of Shipping
Lloyd's Register Office
29 Wellesley Road
Croydon
Surrey   CR0 2AJ
Tel: 01 681 4040
Tlx: 28636 LRISCR G
Fax: 01 681 6814

[1] Also act as purchasing agents.

Appendix 15: Travel services

British Airways travel clinics

Chancellor House Clinic
Shinfield Road
Reading   RG2 7BW
Tel: 0734 311696

101 Cheapside
London   EC2V 6DT
Tel: 01 606 2977

75 Regent Street
London   W1R 7HG
Tel: 01 439 9584

9 Little Newport Street
London   W1R 7HG
Tel: 01 287 2255/3366

Hospital for Tropical Diseases
Travel Clinic
4 St Pancras Way
London   NW1 0PE
Tel: 01 388 9600

19–21 St Mary's Gate
Market Street
Manchester   M1 1PU
Tel: 061 832 3019

16 High Street
Leicester   LE1 5YN
Tel: 0533 516564

The Harrow Health
  Care Centre
84–88 Pinner Road
Harrow
Middlesex   HA1 4LP
Tel: 01 861 1221

The Health Centre
Marsh End Road
Newport Pagnell
Bucks   MK16 8EA
Tel: 0908 211035

Victoria Health Centre
Glasshouse Street
Nottingham   NG1 3LW
Tel: 0602 504058

5/6 Park Terrace
Glasgow   G3 6BY
Tel: 041 332 8010

4 Drumsheugh Gardens
Edinburgh   EH3 7QJ
Tel: 031 226 2794

Rother House Medical Centre
Alcester Road
Stratford upon Avon   CV37 6PP
Tel: 0789 68249

Others

Medical Advisory Service for
  Travellers Abroad (MASTA)
London School of Hygiene and
  Tropical Medicine
Keppel Street
London   WC1
Tel: 01 631 4408

Appendix 16: International services branches – Barclays Bank Plc

(For help with international payments and general trade enquiries)

London branches

City
PO Box 544
54 Lombard Street
London   EC3V 9EX
Tel: 01 621 1888
Tlx: 885176 BBLONA G
Fax: 01 283 7006

Euston Road
Clifton House
83–117 Euston Road
London   NW1 2RA
Tel: 01 388 4262
Tlx: 892462 BAREUS G
Fax: 01 387 1802

Hertsmere House
PO Box 454
Hertsmere House
Marsg Wall
London   E14 9YU
Tel: 01 538 8811
Tlx: 926593/4/5 BARHER G
Fax: 01 538 4301

London Northern
Clifton House
PO Box 1461
83–117 Euston Road
London   NW1 2RG
Tel: 01 388 3886
Tlx: 926171 BARNOR G
Fax: 01 383 4321

Pall Mall
1A Cockspur Street
London   SW1Y 5BG
Tel: 01 930 3131
Tlx: 893514 BARPMA G
Fax: 01 930 0079

Other branches

Birmingham
PO Box 340
45 Church Street
Birmingham   B3 2BZ
Tel: 021 236 4281
Tlx: 336951 BARBI G
Fax: 021 200 1390

Bradford
Pennine House
PO Box 215
45 Well Street
Bradford   BD1 5ED
Tel: 0274 728261
Tlx: 51439 BARBRA G
Fax: 0274 723929

Bristol
PO Box 131
St Stephen's House
Colston Avenue
Bristol   BS99 7DA
Tel: 0272 277705
Tlx: 44333 BARBST G
Fax: 0272 291609

Cardiff
PO Box 31
3rd Floor Windsor Court
3 Windsor Place
Cardiff   CF1 3XL
Tel: 0222 238511
Tlx: 498403 BARCAR G
Fax: 0222 390894

Ipswich
PO Box 11
Crown House
Crown Street
Ipswich   IP1 3JS
Tel: 0473 217944
Tlx: 98113 BARIPS G
Fax: 0473 230854

Liverpool
PO Box 10
4 Water Street
Liverpool   L69 2ET
Tel: 051 2364911
Tlx: 629150 BARLIV G/
        629632 BARLIV G
Fax: 051 2273092

Luton
PO Box 22
28 George Street
Luton   LU1 2HW
Tel: 0582 404321
Tlx: 826401 BARLUT G
Fax: 0582 424241

Manchester
PO Box 543
50 Fountain Street
Manchester   M60 2BU
Tel: 061 8328621
Tlx: 667565 BARMAN G
Fax: 061 8352649

Newcastle upon Tyne
Bamburgh House
Market Street
Newcastle upon Tyne   NE99 1RG
Tel: 091 2329111
Tlx: 53431 BARNEW G
Fax: 091 2615393

Nottingham
PO Box 70
Barclays House
14 Park Row
Nottingham   NG1 6GS
Tel: 0602 412112
Tlx: 37691 BARNOT G
Fax: 0602 476730

Reading
PO Box 44
3–5 King Street
Reading   RG1 2HA
Tel: 0734 585201
Tlx: 849108 BARRED G
Fax: 0734 391162

Sevenoaks
PO Box 3
Beadle House
London Road
Sevenoaks
Kent   TN13 2YH
Tel: 0732 450891
Tlx: 957089 BARSEV G
Fax: 0732 459228

Slough
PO Box 324
Computer Sciences House
Brunel Way
Slough
Berkshire   SL1 1XJ
Tel: 0753 74155
Tlx: 849844 BARSLO G
Fax: 0753 691142

Southampton
PO Box 5
18–20 Cumberland Place
Southampton   SO9 7AF
Tel: 0703 636141
Tlx: 477424 BARSON G
Fax: 0703 211171

Appendix 17: Useful libraries

British Library Business
Information Service
Science Reference Library
25 Southampton Buildings
Chancery Lane
London   WC2A 1AW
Tel: 01 323 7979

City Business Library
Gillett House
55 Basinghall Street
London   EC2V 5BX
Tel: 01 638 8215

Export Market Information
Centre (EMIC)
Department of Trade and Industry
1–19 Victoria Street
London   SW1H OET
Tel: 01 215 5444/5
Tlx: 8811074/5 DTHQ G
Fax: 01 222 2629

The Library
Financial Times Business
Information Service
1 Suffolk Bridge
London   SE1 9HL
Tel: 01 873 3000
Fax: 01 407 5700

Appendix 18: Special publications

General

*British Chambers of Commerce
Service to Exporters Booklet*
Association of British Chambers
of Commerce
Sovereign House
212a Shaftesbury Avenue
London   WC2H 8EW
Tel: 01 240 5831

*Croner's Europe
Croner's Reference Book for
Exporters
Croner's Reference Book for
Importers*
Croner Publications Ltd
Croner House
173 Kingston Road
New Malden
Surrey   KT3 3SS
Tel: 01 942 8966

*Customs Tariff and Overseas
Trade Classification Public
Notices*
HM Customs and Excise
New Kings Beam House
22 Upper Ground
London   SE1 9PJ
Tel: 01 620 1313 or any local
Custom House or Collectors
Office of Customs and Excise

Export Buying Offices Booklet
Export Buying Offices Association
(EXBO)
c/o Portman Ltd
360 Oxford Street
London   W1A 4BA
Tel: 01 493 8141

*Exporter and Forwarder –
The Professional Guide*
British International Freight
Association (BIFA)
Institute of Freight Forwarders
(IFF)
Redfern House,
Browells Lane
Feltham
Middlesex   TW13 7ER
Tel: 01 844 2266

*Hints to Exporters –
Individual Country Booklets*
Department of Trade and Industry
(DTI)
country desks
1–19 Victoria Street
London   SW1H OET
Tel: 01 215 7877

*International Certification and
Approval Schemes Booklet*
BSI Technical Help to Exporters
Linford Wood
Milton Keynes   MK14 6LE
Tel: 0908 220022

*Lloyds Loading List and other
    shipping publications*
Lloyd's of London Press
Sheepen Place
Colchester   CO3 3LP
Tel: 0206 46273

Directories

*ASLIB Directory of Information
    Services in Science,
    Technology and Commerce*
Association for Information
    Management
Information House
20–4 Old Street
London   EC1V 9AP
Tel: 01 253 4488
Tlx: 23667 ASLIBG
Fax: 01 430 0514

Benn's Media Directory
Benn Business Information Services
    Ltd
PO Box 20
Sovereign Way
Tonbridge
Kent   TN9 1RQ

*Brit-line Directory of British
    Databases*
EDI Ltd

*British Exporters
    Association Directory
    of Members*
16 Dartmouth Street
London SW1H 9BL
Tel: 01 222 5419

*Current British Directories
    Directory of British Associations*
CBD Research Ltd
15 Wickham Road
Beckenham
Kent   BR23 2JS

*Directory of British Clothing and
    Textile Importers
Directory of British Importers
The Directory of Export Buyers
    in the UK*
Trade Research Publications

Directory of Directories
Gale Research Company
Book Tower
Detroit   MI 48226
USA

*Directory of International Trade
    Fairs and Exhibitions (MNA)*

*Kelly's Export Services
Kompass Europe*
Information Services Ltd
Windsor Court
East Grinstead
West Sussex   RH19 1XA
Tel: 0342 26972
Tlx: INFSER 95127 G

Whitaker's Almanack
J. Whitaker & Sons Ltd
12 Dyott Street
London   WC1A 1DF
Tel: 01 836 8911

Appendix 19: Bill of exchange form

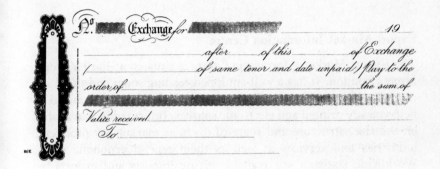

(Printed by kind permission of Tate Freight Forms)

Appendix 20: Sources of market research information

Export Market Information Centre

The Export Market Information Centre is situated at 1–19 Victoria Street, London. It has a well-equipped reading room and there are trained staff available to advise you where to find information and to help you use printed and electronic sources. Information is available on the size, structure and share of overseas markets by products, industries and services as well as their general economic state. Worldwide statistics are available giving imports and exports by product or product type by countries as well as figures on production, prices, employment, transport etc. There is a good selection of overseas trade and telephone directories. The trade directories for Europe and the USA will often give not only information on your manufacturing competitors in each country but also the names and addresses of agents and distributors, some of whom may not carry products directly competitive with yours and hence might be approached to act for you.

Catalogue selling is important in such countries as the USA, and mail order catalogues for different types of consumers are available in the library. A selection of market research reports supplements this and other information. You should check whether any are available covering your general product field.

As might be expected the DTI has its own databases. The Product Data Store (PDS) is on microfilm and contains product information and there is an electronic database of export information called the British Overseas Trade Information System (BOTIS).

Libraries

Local authority central libraries, the British Library's Science Reference Library, libraries belonging to professional institutes, trade associations and educational establishments (e.g. the City Business

Library, London EC2) and the larger Chambers of Commerce (e.g. the London Chamber of Commerce Library, 69 Cannon Street, London) are amongst the many sources of information (see appendix 17). Besides books some of these libraries have UK and foreign magazines and technical journals which can be of help.

In order to find the library you require and in turn the specific directories in your industry or service field it is usually necessary to consult general directories to obtain specific guidance. The *ASLIB Directory of Information Sources in Science, Technology and Commerce* gives guidance on library collections of useful information. A *Directory of Directories* of which there are several published will guide you to the specific trade or service directories in your particular field.

Banks

Barclays Bank, Lloyds Bank and Midland Bank publish free reports on overseas markets. Other leading banks publish regular reports on specific regions or countries in which they operate. Barclays Bank issue a range of reports and publications which give informed comment and views on the international, economic and financial developments covering the economies of over 150 countries (see appendix 16). Banks such as Barclays will obtain an opinion for you on the financial standing of a potential agent or customer. They also have a trade development service which matches importers and exporters.

Department of Trade and Industry services

In addition to the Export Market Information Centre and the regional offices the DTI have a number of other services which provide information and help for exporters. They produce a number of booklets many of which give comprehensive information on selling to the single market. There are also various units at 1–19 Victoria Street which anyone doing market research should get to know.

Country desks

Country desks (see appendix 4) are part of the market information structure in the DTI and cover almost every market in the world.

They are grouped together in branches and their telephone numbers are listed in appendix 4. These desks are in close touch with commercial staff in UK embassies and other posts overseas from whom they receive commercial information of help to exporters. Each desk builds up its own file of information on its markets and this is available to your company usually via your DTI regional office but you may contact the desks direct. If you are researching a particular market tell the country desk what you are doing and what you are trying to find out and you could be pleasantly surprised by the help you receive. The Exports to Europe Branch for example can provide information not only on individual markets but also on import regulations, terms and any special requirements.

Overseas exhibitions and trade missions

The Fairs and Promotions Branch can give you information on overseas exhibitions including international exhibitions in the UK. They also have details of all proposed trade missions. The latter are generally organized by Chambers of Commerce and trade associations.

Overseas and funded business

The World Aid Section provides information on Aid Funds available to developing countries. You can obtain information on indicative projects as well as specific projects. In general small firms are unlikely to seek business directly under aid funds unless they have a specialized product of particular interest to a developing country. More often a small firm will seek business as a subcontractor with the company submitting a tender for an overall project.

European information centres

European information centres (EICs) have been established by the European Commission throughout the single market. They provide European business information and have a dual role to help small firms gain information about the EC and to keep the European Commission informed of the effects of EC policies on small businesses. The centres provide information on EC research and development programmes, public contracts, market intelligence, sources of finance and technical standards and rules.

Language export centres

Language Export (LX) centres (see appendix 10) are normally staffed by members of language and management departments in universities, polytechnics and further education colleges. They are jointly supported by the Professional, Industrial and Commercial Updating Programme (PICKUP) of the Department of Education and Science and the Department of Employment's Training Agency. They provide local firms in their areas with training courses, information and consultancy to assist them in exporting. In particular they offer a combination of language (and cultural) training with business training relating to exporting.

Hints to exporters

The DTI publish a series of booklets for individual markets which are regularly updated. Each booklet contains essential information on currency and exchange regulations, passport and entry formalities, methods of doing business, local holidays, economic factors, social customs and much other useful information. These are available free from the DTI and copies should be obtained for every market you are researching as they will be invaluable when you come to do your field research.

Export Intelligence Service

The DTI receive from all the British diplomatic commercial posts overseas general market information and details of business opportunities. They receive on average 200 business prospects per working day. These are edited, classified and checked and then passed on to Export Opportunities Ltd (EOL) who are a private limited company responsible for the sales and distribution of Export Intelligence Service (EIS) information.

EOL analyse the information in relation to individual company's profiles and needs. Thus any company subscribing to the service can be reasonably confident of receiving business opportunities only for those products and services and for those markets they specify.

Besides the traditional delivery of information by first class post it is also possible to receive it by telex, facsimile, and electronic mail using your computer. Small companies that do not require the information with great urgency will find that the post is probably the cheapest delivery system for their purposes. If your business is highly sophisticated and makes use of electronic equipment then subscribing to Export Network Ltd's on-line database system will provide you with all the EIS information and a great deal more.

A comprehensive on-line database information system for exporters has only become a possibility in recent years. Export Network Ltd have developed the concept which now provides continuously up-dated information under five different headings.

Business opportunities

This section provides export sales leads not only from the EIS but also from some other valuable sources. Sales leads from EIS are contained in the first subsection. Trade Network International is the next subsection containing sales leads from a variety of new sources. This is followed by the government subsection providing information on EC and US government procurements as well as US government awards to help subcontractors. Then comes the Aid and Loan subsection with information from the World Bank's monthly operational summary and on the EC's projects and supply requirements under their Aid and Loans programme. Finally there is a list of foreign agents and importers in Europe and the USA and a list of the export buying houses in the UK.

Country and market research

This section incorporates information from the following.

Hints to Exporters	Methods of doing business in over 100 countries
Technical standards	British Standards Institute information on overseas products standards by country and by product
Exhibitions	Lists of exhibitions sponsored by the British Overseas Trade Board (BOTB) and over 4,000 international trade fairs and exhibitions
UK export licensing	Details of latest requirements

European companies	Information on over 200,000 companies in Europe
Sources of information	Key contacts in the UK and overseas
Export procedures	Information on the technical aspects of exporting

European Community 1992

This section provides extensive information on EC Directives and other matters of interest to exporters. It is explained in detail in the chapter on the single market.

Finance

Each subsection in this section is very important to exporters and provides information on the following subjects which are discussed in more detail in a later chapter.

Foreign exchange	Spot and forward rates for all major currencies
Exchange controls	Information from over 100 countries
Country risk	Assessment of the political and economic risks in trading in over 80 countries
Export credit	Latest terms and conditions for lines of credit
Export Credits Guarantee Department (ECGD) general purpose lines of credit	Lists of countries with outstanding lines of credit
Company status reports	Facility to check the credit worthiness of overseas companies from CCN Systems Ltd

Transport and travel

This section incorporates more essential information needed by an international trader.

Freight forwarders	Information that enables freight forwarders who are used to certain types of product and

	transporting to certain areas to be identified in a company's own locality
Export documentation	Tates Export Guides on the paperwork required for 150 countries
Export documentation updates	Lists of most recent changes in documentation requirements
Visa details	A quick reference for checking visa requirements
World health details	Information a business traveller needs to enable him to remain healthy in different countries

Services

Export Network Ltd provide an electronic mail service so that subscribers can link with each other as well as with the providers of information. The information on sales leads, which can be selected to match a company's profile, can be transmitted to a customer's computer by electronic mail or by automatic fax. Export Network Ltd operate a 'Help Desk', offer demonstrations and training and assist with profiling.

The use of on-line information databases (see appendix 12) is likely to grow rapidly over the next decade as companies discover how to use them to the benefit of their business. There are a number of directories of British databases and these should be consulted to identify which databases are likely to be most useful in your business as an information source. The Export Network Ltd database is the most comprehensive for an exporter but anyone engaged in international trade should also look at the Financial Times Business Information Service and the Profile Information on-line service. These give comprehensive business, company and statistical information based on the coverage in the *Financial Times* and over 60 other leading business publications. They also carry information on the EC Directories.

The Pergamon Financial Data Services and Official Airline Guides give in addition to the airline information, information on major companies worldwide as well as more detailed information on many more companies in the UK, the USA, West Germany and the EC generally. Using worldwide sources it provides text from over 500 newspapers and journals, management and marketing abstracts, specialized information on certain industries and information on technical standards.

The Predicasts family of on-line business information databases contains more than 5 million article abstracts, forecasts, statistics and full text from a broad range of sources in more than 20 countries. It is the largest business information database in North America and if you are investigating database systems for use in your business it should not be overlooked. Both the PROMT and INFORMAT databases contain extensive information on the single market. Predicast Databases can be accessed and searched via the Dialog and Data-Star host systems.

Kompass Online (Reed Information Services Limited) provides information on UK and European companies. Reed International Plc subsidiaries also publish directories such as *Kelly's Export Services* and *Kompass Europe*. A number of organizations including some Chambers of Commerce such as the London Chamber are acting as on-line information database brokers. They are linked to a number of different databases and for a fee SMEs can obtain information from the Chambers who will search the databases for them.

Glossary

ad valorem duty Duty based on a percentage of the cargo value.

aircraft manifest List of individual consignments on an aircraft.

air way-bill Air freight consignment document made out by or on behalf of the shipper. It is a document of title.

aligned forms Series of forms designed so that information appears on each form in the pack as required by recipients.

arbitration Method of settling disputes which is usually binding on the parties involved. Many international trade contracts contain arbitration clauses stipulating the method of arbitration.

banker's draft A draft drawn by one bank on another bank in favour of a third party. Drafts should comply with the rules for cheques in the country in which they are payable.

bill of exchange An unconditional order in writing, addressed by one party or person to another, signed by the party giving it, requiring the party to whom it is addressed to pay on demand or at a fixed or determinable future time a sum of money to, or to the order of, a specified party or the bearer.

bill of lading A receipt of goods placed on board a ship, signed by the person or agent who contracts to carry them. It states the terms on which the goods are carried and is a document of title.

carnet A document usually obtained from Chambers of Commerce which allows the temporary importation without payment of duty of commercial samples, exhibition materials and similar goods.

certificate of origin A document identifying the goods shipped and expressly stating where the goods were manufactured, e.g. originated. They are usually certified by Chambers of Commerce.

clean bill of lading   A bill of lading with no additional clauses declaring a defective state of the goods or packing.

consignment note   A document which usually states the terms under which goods are carried. It normally accompanies the goods throughout transit.

consolidation   The system of sending a number of consignments from various consignees to various consignors as one overall consignment.

customs entry   The form of which the importer gives details of the goods for customs clearance.

demurrage   The money paid by the shipper or the seller for delays in loading, discharging or occupying space at a port or warehouse beyond a specified period. It usually arises from customs clearance delays.

del credere   The agent's guarantee to his principal for the solvency of the parties to whom he makes sales. It is included in agency agreements when required.

documentary collection   The exporter's bank sends the appropriate documents including that of title to the importer's bank. The importer usually receives the documents in exchange for payment or acceptance of a term bill of exchange.

documentary letter of credit   Document whereby at the buyer's request his bank authorizes the exporter to draw payment by a specified date for a particular shipment against the presentation of accurate and detailed documents in accordance with the terms of the credit.

exchange rate   Price of one currency in terms of another.

export licence   A document which grants permission to export specified goods within a certain time.

factor   A company which administers the sales ledger, pays the exporter and collects payment from the importer or his agent/bank.

force majeure   A clause limiting the responsibilities of suppliers and shippers under certain circumstances. Usually this clause is included in the contract conditions.

forfaiter   The forfaiting company purchases for cash a seller's receivables. The seller receives payment from the forfaiter and loses his right to the future payment. The forfaiter collects payment from the buyer or his agent/bank.

forwarding agent   The party responsible for the arrangements for importing/exporting cargo. Usually described as a freight forwarder.

groupage   System of sending various packages from different consignees under one agent to a common destination. It is also known as consolidation.

indemnity   Compensation for loss, damage or injury.

insurance certificate   A certificate that is proof that insurance for a particular shipment has been arranged.

intermodal   Carriage by various means of transport, e.g. air, sea, road and rail.

letter of indemnity   A document indemnifying the agent or shipper from any risks or claims that may arise through the use of an incorrect 'clean' bill of lading.

manifest   List of cargo on board a ship.

market price   The price at which a product would sell if sold on the open market.

negotiable bill of lading   A bill of lading that can be transferred or endorsed.

Pre-entry   The process of lodging documents with the customs prior to the shipment or arrival of the goods.

revolving credits   A system whereby the importer arranges with his bank for a certain sum to be available so that payment can be made for each shipment under a series of shipments usually under one contract.

seaway bill   A non-negotiable document (that lists the goods) which is evidence of a contract for the carriage of goods by sea.

shipping documents Documents that enable shipments to be sent or received.

trans-shipment The process of transferring cargo from one transport mode to another.

wharfage The fees paid for using a wharf or accommodation at a wharf.